Small Beads, Big Jewellery

Jean Power

Search Press

A QUARTO BOOK

Published in 2014 by
Search Press Ltd
Wellwood
North Farm Road
Tunbridge Wells
Kent TN2 3DR

Reprinted 2014

ISBN 978-1-78221-021-4

QUAR:MGBE

Conceived, designed and produced by
Quarto Publishing plc
The Old Brewery
6 Blundell Street
London N7 9BH

Senior project editor: Corinne Masciocchi
Art editor: Jackie Palmer
Designer: Austin Taylor
Photographer for styled projects: Lydia Evans
Photographer for cutouts: Phil Wilkins
Illustrator: Kuo Kang Chen
Art director: Caroline Guest
Creative director: Moira Clinch
Publisher: Paul Carslake

Colour separation in Singapore by Pica Digital Pte Limited
Printed in China by 1010 Printing International Limited

10 9 8 7 6 5 4 3 2

Contents

Projects   24

Foreword

Welcome to *Small Beads, Big Jewellery*! Within these pages, my love of beading and creating bold and modern jewellery combine to bring you 30 dazzling projects from around the world. There is something for everyone: from simple bangles to glitzy evening necklaces (and everything in between), you'll find yourself wanting to make the whole lot! When designing the projects for this book, I wanted to create contemporary, wearable jewellery suitable for all ages. But most of all, I wanted to design unique pieces that can be worn with pride and elicit a few envious glances at the same time!

For those new to beadweaving, you'll find clear, easy-to-follow stitch techniques at the beginning of each section, so that you can gain comprehensive knowledge of each one before embarking on the projects made using those techniques. You'll also find constructive hints and tips dotted throughout, to help you achieve the results you want.

Excitingly, this book also features projects by ten very talented designers from around the world who I have personally selected to showcase their unique styles and expertise. I hope each project within the pages of this book will inspire you not only to further develop your love of beading, but also to encourage you to create your very own masterpieces.

Jean Power

About this book

Beaders' world

This section introduces you to the world of beaders and also to the designers who, with Jean, have created the projects in this book.

This section is peppered with useful information for beginner beaders wanting to join the community.

In their own words: each designer describes how beading brings them joy, and shares handy tips and tricks of the trade.

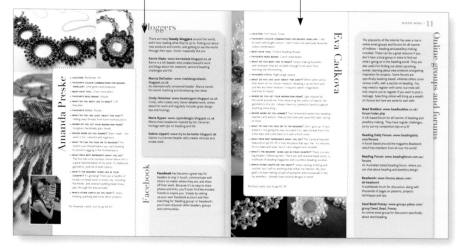

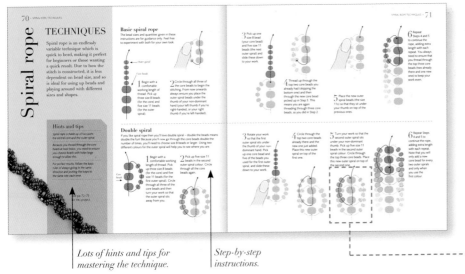

Lots of hints and tips for mastering the technique.

Step-by-step instructions.

Techniques

Each stitch technique is presented with core instructions, followed by projects that put that technique into practice.

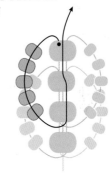

HOW TO READ THE BEAD DIAGRAMS

The thread is represented by a black line with an arrow, showing the direction of travel. Beads that are being worked have a dark outline and are in a stronger colour than those that have already been worked. The black dot on a bead shows the last bead worked.

Projects

Four or five projects accompany each technique, with the beginner projects first.

Skill level is shown: projects range from easy, to intermediate, to advanced.

PROJECT COLOURWAY
This neat little device focuses on colour and shows why a colourway is successful by identifying the colour combination used in the finished piece.

The tools and materials list ensures you have everything you need to make the project.

Techniques used are listed here.

The dimensions of the finished project are supplied.

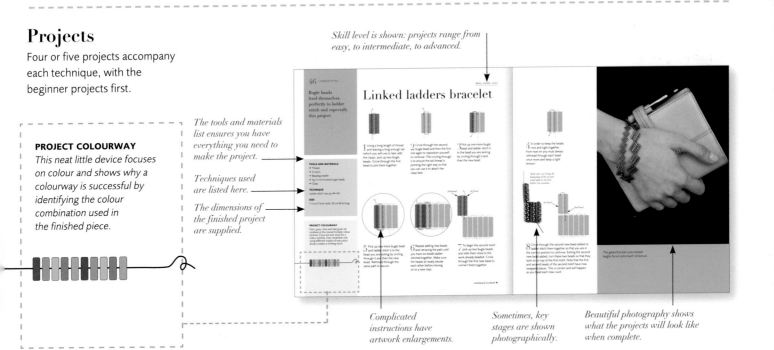

Complicated instructions have artwork enlargements.

Sometimes, key stages are shown photographically.

Beautiful photography shows what the projects will look like when complete.

Beaders' world

While beading has been a craft enjoyed by many over hundreds of years, it is over the past decade that it has really exploded. Thanks to the internet, in particular social networking sites and forums, beaders from around the world can now come together to share their love of beads and beading. Instant access to pictures of work created by someone halfway around the world means that styles and influences bounce back and forth, and ideas are shared quickly and easily. These ideas then spread to local beading groups and classes, or among friends, and take off in many different directions. Many beaders also blog and share their ideas and current projects, which receive feedback and advice from the online community, resulting in more interesting work. On these pages, you get to meet the beading designers whose work features in this book.

Jean Power

- **LOCATION:** London, UK.
- **FAVOURITE COLOUR COMBINATIONS FOR BEADED JEWELLERY:** Anything, so long as it shouts! Whatever colours I use, I always make sure to use lots of matt beads.
- **MUST-HAVE TOOLS:** My glasses and good thread.
- **FAVOURITE BEAD BRAND:** Miyuki – I adore delicas.
- **WHAT DO YOU MOST LIKE TO MAKE?** I love making jewellery that has more than one function, such as a bracelet that can be turned into a necklace. Making something interchangeable can be a challenge, but I enjoy that.
- **FAVOURITE STITCH:** Peyote – my brain seems to think in this stitch.
- **WHAT DO YOU LIKE LEAST ABOUT THIS CRAFT?** How long it takes to make something – I long for speedier results!
- **WHERE DO YOU GET YOUR INSPIRATION FROM?** Primarily from the beads – thinking of ways to show them off and get them to do what I want is my main inspiration.
- **WHOSE WORK DO YOU ADMIRE?** So many, but Suzanne Golden, Merle Berelowitz, Gabriella van Diepen, Pat Neeve and Sue Maguire all come to mind.
- **WHAT TIP CAN YOU PASS ON TO THE READERS?** Experiment! At first it can seem impossible to alter projects, but wonderful things can happen by approaching them with the mindset of 'I wonder what would happen if...'
- **WHAT PIECE BEST REPRESENTS WHAT YOU DO?** I am best known for my geometric work, such as some of the pieces in this book, and it is this work that I love doing most.
- **WHAT'S THE BEADERS' SCENE LIKE IN YOUR COUNTRY?** Very mixed. When I first started beading it was a very closed community of mainly ladies of a certain age from an embroidery background, but the internet, especially Facebook, and new beading magazines have changed that. It has become much more open and sharing, with new blood and fresh ideas coming in all the time.
- **WHICH OTHER CRAFTS DO YOU ENJOY?** I love wirework and chain maille, as well as tapestry, wax carving, felt-making and polymer clay... anything I can get my hands on!

Classes

Beading classes, whether followed online or taken in person, are a great way to learn about the craft. You'll not only get to learn the techniques, you'll also pick up so many gems of knowledge from both the teacher and other students. It can be worth doing a class just to spend fun time with other beaders, learn how they bead and any tips they have, discover new shops and groups in conversation, see the same project in different colours, and make new friends who support and encourage your beading habit!

Many **competitions**, both online and around the world, have sprung up and these are a great way to test yourself, show off your work, get feedback from others and potentially win a prize! They can be small challenges on a forum with no prize, or a large international competition with sponsors and big prizes (with an entry fee). You may be required to bead a piece that fits a particular theme or uses a particular material, or you may be able to create anything you choose. Sometimes you have to send in your piece, but often a photo is all that is required. Whatever the format, my top five tips are:

1. Read the rules! It might seem obvious, but getting a small detail wrong can affect your chances of winning. Make sure you know what the closing date is, how to enter and exactly what is required.

2. Submit good photographs. This can be the hardest thing to get right, but even if you're not a world-class snapper, these guidelines will help. Always make sure:
- your photographs fit the criteria you are given
- the background isn't too distracting – your piece should be the focus
- all of the work is shown, so no cropping
- the lighting is good enough so that all the details can be seen
- the pictures are sharp and in focus.

3. Take care of the small details. Little things like stray threads, broken beads or badly finished work can make a big difference when judges make their choices, so make sure your work doesn't lose because of a minor point.

4. Be original. We're all influenced by our surroundings, but don't be tempted to copy someone else's work – the judges will be looking out for this!

5. Relax! View the competition as a personal challenge and don't put pressure on yourself to make something record-breaking. See whether you can work to a deadline, fit specific criteria or simply get around to entering, and pat yourself on the back if you achieve this.

Amanda Preske

- **LOCATION:** Rochester, NY.
- **FAVOURITE COLOUR COMBINATIONS FOR BEADED JEWELLERY:** Lime green and turquoise.
- **MUST-HAVE TOOL:** Chain-nose pliers.
- **FAVOURITE BEAD BRAND:** Miyuki.
- **WHAT DO YOU MOST LIKE TO MAKE?** Cuff bracelets.
- **FAVOURITE STITCH:** Peyote.
- **WHAT DO YOU LIKE LEAST ABOUT THIS CRAFT?** Hiding warp threads from loom-worked pieces.
- **WHERE DO YOU GET YOUR INSPIRATION FROM?** Gorgeous handmade glass beads.
- **WHOSE WORK DO YOU ADMIRE?** Sherri Haab – her work is fun, colourful and ingenious.
- **WHAT TIP CAN YOU PASS ON TO READERS?** Pre-stretch your thread before you start beading to prevent sagging in the finished piece.
- **WHAT PIECE BEST REPRESENTS WHAT YOU DO?** The five-link circle necklace shown above left is a great representation of my work. It's balanced, geometric, and full of bold colours.
- **WHAT'S THE BEADERS' SCENE LIKE IN YOUR COUNTRY?** It's growing! There are a handful of locally run bead stores in every city, including Rochester, and several travelling bead shows pass through the area annually.
- **WHICH OTHER CRAFTS DO YOU ENJOY?** I enjoy knitting, painting and home décor projects.

For Amanda's work, turn to pp.64–67.

Bloggers

There are many **beady bloggers** around the world, and I love reading what they're up to, finding out about new products and events, and getting to see the world through their eyes. Some I especially like are:

Kerrie Slade: www.kerrieslade.blogspot.co.uk
Kerrie is a UK beader who creates beautiful work and blogs about her creations, personal beading challenges and life.

Marcia DeCoster: www.maddesignsbeads.blogspot.co.uk
An internationally renowned beader, Marcia travels the world, teaching and developing new ideas.

Cindy Holsclaw: www.beadorigami.blogspot.co.uk
Cindy, who creates very clever detailed work, writes about her work and regularly includes great design tips and musings.

Maria Rypan: www.rypandesigns.blogspot.co.uk
Maria mixes beadwork inspired by her Ukrainian heritage with tips on beading and life.

Sabine Lippert: www.try-to-be-better.blogspot.de
Sabine is a German beader who creates intricate and ornate work.

Facebook

Facebook has become a great way for beaders to stay in touch, communicate with others no matter where they are, and show off their work. Because it's so easy to share photos and links, you'll soon find like-minded friends to inspire you. Simply by setting up your own Facebook account and then searching for 'beading group' or 'beadwork', you'll soon discover other beaders, groups and communities.

Eva Cadkova

- **LOCATION:** Fort Hood, Texas.
- **FAVOURITE COLOUR COMBINATIONS FOR BEADED JEWELLERY:** I like to work with bright colours. I don't have one particular favourite colour combination.
- **MUST-HAVE TOOL:** Fireline beading thread.
- **FAVOURITE BEAD BRAND:** Czech seed beads.
- **WHAT DO YOU MOST LIKE TO MAKE?** I enjoy making bracelets and necklaces that are versatile enough to be worn from morning into the evening.
- **FAVOURITE STITCH:** Right-angle weave.
- **WHAT DO YOU LIKE LEAST ABOUT THIS CRAFT?** When other artists look down on my chosen medium. Beading is an art form and just like any other medium, it requires talent, imagination and time to master.
- **WHERE DO YOU GET YOUR INSPIRATION FROM?** I get inspired by the world around me, from observing the colours of nature, the geometrics of a city. I always have my camera to hand to capture anything interesting.
- **WHOSE WORK DO YOU ADMIRE?** Two renowned masterclass beading teachers and authors, Marcia DeCoster and Laura McCabe, spring to mind.
- **WHAT TIP CAN YOU PASS ON TO THE READERS?** Don't give up. If your project is not going the way you want it to, take a break from it for a few days and come back to it with a fresh mind.
- **WHAT PIECE BEST REPRESENTS WHAT YOU DO?** The Caroline bracelet featured on pp.92–95 is truly the piece that says 'me'. It's not only fun to make and wear, but it's also elegant and versatile.
- **WHAT'S THE BEADERS' SCENE LIKE IN YOUR COUNTRY?** There is a very big beaders' following here. There are well-stocked bead stores, a multitude of beading magazines and countless beading societies.
- **WHICH OTHER CRAFTS DO YOU ENJOY?** I enjoy sewing, knitting and crochet, but I will try anything that strikes my interest. My next goal is to learn tatting (a type of lacework) and incorporate it into my jewellery. I already have several designs in mind!

For Eva's work, turn to pp.92–95.

Online groups and forums

The popularity of the internet has seen a rise in online email groups and forums for all manner of hobbies – beading and jewellery-making included. These can be a great resource if you don't have a local group or store to find out what's going on in the beading world. They are also useful for finding out about upcoming events, learning about new products and getting inspiration for projects. Some forums are specifically beading-based, whereas others cover various crafts, with a section on beading. You may need to register with some, but most will only require you to register if you want to post a message. Searching online will bring up a wealth of choices but here are some to start with:

Bead Buddies: www.beadbuddies.co.uk/forum/index.php
A UK-based forum for all manner of beading and jewellery-making. They have regular challenges, so try out my competition tips on p.9!

Beading Daily Forum: www.beadingdaily.com/forums
A forum based around the magazine *Beadwork*, which has members from all over the world.

Beading Forum: www.beadingforum.com.au/forums
An Australian-based beading forum, where you can chat about beading and jewellery design.

Beadwork: www.forums.about.com/ab-beadwork
A worldwide forum for discussion, along with thousands of pages on patterns, projects, techniques and tips.

Seed Bead Frenzy: www.groups.yahoo.com/group/Seed_Bead_Frenzy
An online email group for discussion specifically about seed beading.

Maria Lindemann

- **LOCATION:** Copenhagen, Denmark.
- **FAVOURITE COLOUR COMBINATIONS FOR BEADED JEWELLERY:** I can't really choose a favourite combo as I love all colours.
- **MUST-HAVE TOOLS:** Needles, threads and beads – that's it.
- **FAVOURITE BEAD BRAND:** Miyuki and delica seed beads.
- **WHAT DO YOU MOST LIKE TO MAKE?** Once I've created a new pattern, the most exciting part for me is making the prototype and seeing the result in the flesh.
- **FAVOURITE STITCHES:** Brick and peyote.
- **WHAT DO YOU LIKE LEAST ABOUT THIS CRAFT?** Everything about beading is good – I love all of it! The only thing I can say I least like is making a lot of the same patterns in the same colours in one go – that can get a bit boring.
- **WHERE DO YOU GET YOUR INSPIRATION FROM?** All around me.
- **WHOSE WORK DO YOU ADMIRE?** I have seen a lot of gorgeous work from various beaders on Etsy and other places online – I admire all of them!
- **WHAT TIP CAN YOU PASS ON TO READERS?** If following instructions for a project, read them all the way through first; that way you're less likely to make a mistake.
- **WHAT PIECE BEST REPRESENTS WHAT YOU DO?** My beaded owls (see pp.62–63) and other animals are probably the pieces that represent me best. I like my designs to have a bit of humor and cuteness.
- **WHAT'S THE BEADERS' SCENE LIKE IN YOUR COUNTRY?** I recently came across a girl who uses the same kind of beads as I do (delicas) – that's the only time I've seen this kind of beading in my country.
- **WHICH OTHER CRAFTS DO YOU ENJOY?** I like to knit, crochet and sew.

For Maria's work, turn to pp.62–63.

Shirley Lim

- **LOCATION:** Singapore, Singapore.
- **FAVOURITE COLOUR COMBINATIONS FOR BEADED JEWELLERY:** Gold, silver and matt beads.
- **MUST-HAVE TOOLS:** Needles and a pair of scissors.
- **FAVOURITE BEAD BRAND:** Miyuki.
- **WHAT DO YOU MOST LIKE TO MAKE?** Necklaces, earrings and beaded beads.
- **FAVOURITE STITCHES:** Peyote and herringbone.
- **WHAT DO YOU LIKE LEAST ABOUT THIS CRAFT?** I like all aspects of beading!
- **WHERE DO YOU GET YOUR INSPIRATION FROM?** Historical art pieces, fantasy ideas.
- **WHOSE WORK DO YOU ADMIRE?** Cynthia Rutledge and Laura McCabe.
- **WHAT TIP CAN YOU PASS ON TO THE READERS?** Use good-quality beads as you are, essentially, making a piece of art.
- **WHAT PIECE BEST REPRESENTS WHAT YOU DO?** I haven't got one yet.
- **WHAT'S THE BEADERS' SCENE LIKE IN YOUR COUNTRY?** It's only a small community, so not much is happening locally at present.
- **WHICH OTHER CRAFTS DO YOU ENJOY?** Knitting, crochet and sewing.

For Shirley's work, turn to pp.138–41.

Shelley Nybakke

- **LOCATION:** Normal, Illinois.
- **FAVOURITE COLOUR COMBINATIONS FOR BEADED JEWELLERY:** Gold and turquoise, or ivory and black.
- **MUST-HAVE TOOL:** Fireline beading thread.
- **FAVOURITE BEAD BRAND:** Any Japanese seed beads, Swarovski crystals, pearls and Czech fire-polished beads.
- **WHAT DO YOU MOST LIKE TO MAKE?** Wide bracelets.
- **FAVOURITE STITCH:** Right-angle weave.
- **WHAT DO YOU LIKE LEAST ABOUT THIS CRAFT?** There is nothing I dislike about beading, other than sometimes my passion to do nothing but bead interferes with real life!
- **WHERE DO YOU GET YOUR INSPIRATION FROM?** Shapes. I envisage a shape for a piece and see if I can make it happen. Sometimes it works, sometimes it doesn't!
- **WHOSE WORK DO YOU ADMIRE?** NanC Meinhardt has always been my beading idol. She is the Elvis of the beading world!
- **WHAT TIP CAN YOU PASS ON TO READERS?** If you're wondering 'What would happen if...', then go ahead and try it. That is advice I received from NanC Meinhardt and it has been invaluable to me.
- **WHAT PIECE BEST REPRESENTS WHAT YOU DO?** I think my 'Simply Marvelous, Darling' cuff, shown below, is my best work. It's very elegant and can have so many different looks, depending on what embellishment you use. My 'Until I Can Breathe Again' necklace helped me through a very bad period in my life after divorce and saved me from too much craziness due to the meditative, relaxing process of making it. I love wearing it as it's such fun!
- **WHAT'S THE BEADERS' SCENE LIKE IN YOUR COUNTRY?** The beaders in the US are wonderful, and very willing to share ideas and knowledge.
- **WHICH OTHER CRAFTS DO YOU ENJOY?** Knitting, needlepoint and painting.
- **WHAT IS YOUR FAVOURITE ASPECT OF BEADING?** The wonderful beaders I have met all over the world. Thanks to beading, I now have truly international friends. Also it has given me the opportunity to travel much more and see places I never would have had a chance to see. And patience; beading has taught me great patience.

For Shelley's work, turn to pp.112–15.

Local groups

There are now **local beading groups** all over the world – there may be one right near you. If there isn't, why not set up your own? All you need is a suitable venue and at least one other person, and you've got a group going! Some groups are large and formal with set meeting places, speakers and maybe even bead sellers, whereas others are smaller and have informal meetings once a month in a member's home, local bead store or even a café to bead and catch up. How you run your group is up to you and the other members. If you are looking for beaders to join you, why not ask your local bead society, put a notice in a local bead store, put the word out on beading forums, contact a beading magazine in your country or put a request on Facebook. Pretty soon you'll have them flocking!

Arantxa A.

- **LOCATION:** Vitoria-Gasteiz, Álava, Spain.
- **FAVOURITE COLOUR COMBINATIONS FOR BEADED JEWELLERY:** Bronze and royal blue.
- **MUST-HAVE TOOL:** A needle – I can't go anywhere without a needle!
- **FAVOURITE BEAD BRAND:** Toho, without a doubt.
- **WHAT DO YOU MOST LIKE TO MAKE?** Bracelets and rings, because necklaces are too long and I don't like making earrings – I hate making the same piece twice!
- **FAVOURITE STITCH:** Right-angle weave.
- **WHAT DO YOU LIKE LEAST ABOUT THIS CRAFT?** Tidying and sorting my work table. Suddenly, seed beads seem to multiply themselves...
- **WHERE DO YOU GET YOUR INSPIRATION FROM?** From the internet, which is full of amazing artisans.
- **WHOSE WORK DO YOU ADMIRE?** Dori Csengeri shocked me the first time I saw her soutache jewellery. In my opinion, Jean Power is the peyote queen. And if we're talking about bead embroidery, then Sherry Serafini is the guru.
- **WHAT TIP CAN YOU PASS ON TO THE READERS?** Try again. I've been making jewellery for fifteen years and 'trial and error' is the only way of improving. You must try, try and try again until you are satisfied with the end result. If you don't like it or can't get it quite right, just give it another go – you'll get there in the end.
- **WHAT PIECE BEST REPRESENTS WHAT YOU DO?** The Alloga pendant, bottom right. It is stitched on a filigree. When I started making this pendant I had no idea what the end result would be. I had the filigree and I selected a combination of bright beads, took the needle, and started sewing the beads on the filigree. Each row came naturally and without premeditation. I love the freedom of just adding beads without using a pattern.
- **WHAT'S THE BEADERS' SCENE LIKE IN YOUR COUNTRY?** Beaders are improving in leaps and bounds in Spain. There are lots of incredible Spanish beaders, all with their own unique style.
- **WHICH OTHER CRAFTS DO YOU ENJOY?** Apart from beading, I love soutache jewellery (a type of embroidered jewellery), chain maille and macramé. And I dream of the day when I'll have enough time to experiment with wire wrapping and metal clay.

For Arantxa's work, turn to pp.30–33.

Bead societies

There are a multitude of **bead societies and guilds** that support beaders. Some may organise regular meetings, while others have newsletters and projects for you to make. All are a great resource for finding out about events and classes in your area, and meeting other beaders local to you. You can find a list of societies around the world at: **http://bnb.jewelrymakingmagazines.com/groups.aspx**.

Mortira Natasha van Pelt

- **LOCATION:** British Columbia, Canada.

- **FAVOURITE COLOUR COMBINATIONS FOR BEADED JEWELLERY:** I'm head over heels for just about any combination that includes a bright, sour green: chartreuse, light olive or even neon green. My all-time favourite combination is cobalt blue with lime – it never fails to cheer me up or inspire a new design.

- **MUST-HAVE TOOL:** My collection of bead cups and trays. I use a little set of metal coasters to hold the beads that I'm working with. Any tray or dish will do, so long as it has enough of a lip to keep the beads in place and is shallow enough for needling up beads.

- **FAVOURITE BEAD BRAND:** I place a lot of restrictions on the type of beads that I use in my work, so I can't say that I love all beads equally, but choosing a single favourite is tricky. Each style and make has its own appealing qualities. If I had to choose just one bead brand to use, I'd go with Preciosa Czech seed beads. They're gorgeous, good quality and affordable.

- **WHAT DO YOU MOST LIKE TO MAKE?** I'm always happiest when I'm making necklaces, especially collars and lariats. Of all the jewellery styles one can create, necklaces are the most versatile in terms of fit and wearability.

- **FAVOURITE STITCHES:** Herringbone weave and variations are what I most often turn to when designing a totally new piece, or looking for a comfort project. I also have great affection for the versatility of right-angle weave, and the elegant collars that can be created with netting.

- **WHAT DO YOU LIKE LEAST ABOUT THIS CRAFT?** If I had to pick one 'con' of beading, I would have to say weaving in threads. It's usually the most dreaded part of any project and often left until the last possible minute.

- **WHERE DO YOU GET YOUR INSPIRATION FROM?** Like many beaders, I get a lot of ideas from nature – the things I see around me, as well as exotic patterns and colours from around the world. My biggest source of inspiration is ancient Egyptian art and mythology – though anything reminiscent of Africa or the Mediterranean is welcome in my workspace. Bold colours, stripes and organic textures are the elements I most often mix to get a design that I really love.

- **WHOSE WORK DO YOU ADMIRE?** I'm a big fan of Diane Fitzgerald. Her work is always so stunning and seems to stem from a pure love of beads. When Diane creates a project for a new bead type, she makes it look as if those beads were manufactured just for her. I hope one day to be as talented and versatile as Diane.

- **WHAT TIP CAN YOU PASS ON TO READERS?** To be happiest in beading, make what you love. There will always be trends in beadwork and jewellery design, fancy new techniques, or bead types that seem to be everywhere – try anything once, but keep only those materials and techniques that make you relish sitting down to bead.

- **WHAT PIECE BEST REPRESENTS WHAT YOU DO?** My signature design changes all the time, evolving along with my skills and tastes. Right now, I'd like to think that netted collars in striking colours will be a lasting part of my bead persona.

- **WHAT'S THE BEADERS' SCENE LIKE IN YOUR COUNTRY?** Canada has a wonderful foundation of crafting and fine arts, with each region's cultural influence creating a fascinating tapestry. I've met a lot of very talented Canadian beaders online, though not many beadweavers here on the West Coast.

- **WHICH OTHER CRAFTS DO YOU ENJOY?** I've been so engrossed with beadweaving for the past several years that I've almost forgotten how to do anything else! I'm occasionally drawn to acrylic painting, paper collage and mixed media.

For Mortira's work, turn to pp.130–33.

Justine Standaert

- **LOCATION:** Oaxaca City, Mexico.

- **FAVOURITE COLOUR COMBINATIONS FOR BEADED JEWELLERY:** The bright Mexican colours and colour combinations are incredible: red and turquoise, green and purple, yellow and red, etc. They brighten up everything!

- **MUST-HAVE TOOLS:** Crochet hook and tweezers.

- **FAVOURITE BEAD BRAND:** I'm not into specific brands. I prefer to look for natural, organic, colourful beads from all over. You can find the most beautiful beads in the least-expected places!

- **WHAT DO YOU MOST LIKE TO MAKE?** I like to take existing techniques and designs, give them a different twist and turn them into something else. I love to make jewellery out of uncommon materials such as acai beads, or I get inspired by classic jewellery and try to make the 'funky' version. I really enjoy the process of playing with beads and trying new things.

- **FAVOURITE STITCHES:** My favourite stitch is right-angle weave, though I also like peyote.

- **WHAT DO YOU LIKE LEAST ABOUT THIS CRAFT?** Nothing I can think of at the moment, I enjoy the craft 100 per cent. The boring part is the administrative tasks that have to be done in order to run a craft business, but then again, I don't mind – so long as I can make jewellery for a living, I am happy!

- **WHERE DO YOU GET YOUR INSPIRATION FROM?** Definitely from the country I live in, Mexico. The colours, the vibes, the fiestas and siestas, the handmade way of life, the music, the dancing and the overall happiness.

- **WHOSE WORK DO YOU ADMIRE?** I really admire Nikki Couppee. Her jewellery is just amazing – colourful, crazy, unique, handcrafted and simply adorable!

- **WHAT TIP CAN YOU PASS ON TO READERS?** Enjoy every step of the process – from choosing the colours of your beads to wearing the finished piece. Take it slowly and just enjoy.

- **WHAT PIECE BEST REPRESENTS WHAT YOU DO?** Probably the red multistrand açai necklace pictured below. This necklace marked the beginning of my beading adventure! I made that necklace for the first time many years ago. I used to sell it on a stall and an American jewellery designer passed by, bought it and ordered more. That's how and why I started to make more of them in other colours and designs, and then began selling them online. They have been an amazing success ever since!

- **WHAT'S THE BEADERS' SCENE LIKE IN YOUR COUNTRY?** In Mexico there are lots of beaders, mostly in the Huichol style.

- **WHICH OTHER CRAFTS DO YOU ENJOY?** I also make silver jewellery and jewellery using recycled materials such as bottle caps and mirrors. I also enjoy painting, drawing and photography.

For Justine's work, turn to pp.108–11.

Juanita Carlos (Jaycee)

- **LOCATIONS:** Johannesburg, South Africa, and Sunshine Coast, Australia.
- **FAVOURITE COLOUR COMBINATIONS FOR BEADED JEWELLERY:** Cream, gold and pink.
- **MUST-HAVE TOOL:** Imagination.
- **FAVOURITE BEAD BRAND:** Miyuki, which are Japanese seed beads, and Toho beads.
- **WHAT DO YOU MOST LIKE TO MAKE?** Pearl and crystal bracelets.
- **FAVOURITE STITCH:** Triangle weave and netting stitch.
- **WHAT DO YOU LIKE LEAST ABOUT THIS CRAFT?** Starting over when I've made a mistake.
- **WHERE DO YOU GET YOUR INSPIRATION FROM?** Everything around me.
- **WHOSE WORK DO YOU ADMIRE?** Zulu beadwork.
- **WHAT TIP CAN YOU PASS ON TO THE READERS?** Persevere – practice makes perfect!
- **WHAT PIECE BEST REPRESENTS WHAT YOU DO?** The pearl filigree necklace, shown above, as I feel it depicts my own unique design style.
- **WHAT'S THE BEADERS' SCENE LIKE IN YOUR COUNTRY?** It's not as popular as in the US and Europe.
- **WHICH OTHER CRAFTS DO YOU ENJOY?** Painting, crochet and leathercraft.

For Juanita's work, turn to pp.134–37.

Debbie van Tonder

- **LOCATION:** Cape Town, South Africa.
- **FAVOURITE COLOUR COMBINATIONS FOR BEADED JEWELLERY:** Brown and gold.
- **MUST-HAVE TOOL:** Needle.
- **FAVOURITE BEAD BRAND:** Miyuki and Tila beads in particular. These Japanese beads are square and flat with two parallel holes running side by side, and come in all sorts of colours and finishes.
- **WHAT DO YOU MOST LIKE TO MAKE?** Bangles and bracelets.
- **FAVOURITE STITCH:** Peyote.
- **WHAT DO YOU LIKE LEAST ABOUT THIS CRAFT?** Running out of thread.
- **WHERE DO YOU GET YOUR INSPIRATION FROM?** The peace and quiet of my surroundings.
- **WHOSE WORK DO YOU ADMIRE?** All crafters.
- **WHAT TIP CAN YOU PASS ON TO READERS?** Be patient.
- **WHAT PIECE BEST REPRESENTS WHAT YOU DO?** The Zoe bangles, shown above, made using Tila beads. Most of my designs are worked from Tila beads, which I use to create a base structure and to add embellishment.
- **WHAT'S THE BEADERS' SCENE LIKE IN YOUR COUNTRY?** There's not a huge amount going on as I live in a small coastal village.
- **WHICH OTHER CRAFT DO YOU ENJOY?** Sewing.

For Debbie's work, turn to pp.104–07.

All the essentials

One of the best parts of beading is collecting all the beads and materials you need. Here is where you can combine the needs for the project with your personal style and taste to create something that's unique to you. Whether it is choosing beads or the small metal components (known as findings) such as clasps, which are so essential to your work, knowing the basics about them will help you when deciding what to buy.

BEADS

The most important components for beading are, of course, beads. These come in a wide range of makes, colours, shapes and sizes, so experiment and have fun with your choices.

Size 15 seed beads

Seed beads

Seed beads are shaped like a ring doughnut and come in a wide range of sizes, but the most commonly used are sizes 15, 11, 8 and 6. The smaller the number, the larger the bead.

Size 6 seed beads

Cylinder beads

'Cylinder beads' is the generic term used for beads that are shaped like a cut section of glass tube with flat ends. The accurate sizing of these Japanese beads makes them perfect for structural pieces.

Cylinder beads

Bicone crystals

Crystal beads come in various shapes, but the most commonly used in beading are bicones. Available in various sizes and in a multitude of colours and coatings, they fit together nicely and bring an element of bling to your work.

Bicone crystals in a variety of sizes and finishes

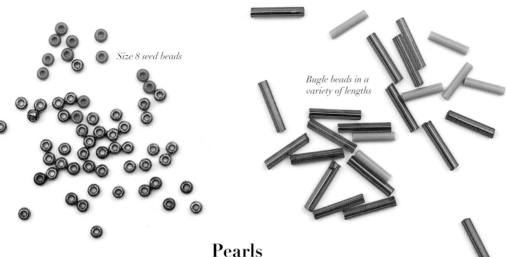

Size 8 seed beads

Bugle beads in a variety of lengths

Bugle beads

Bugles are long, straight beads cut from lengths of glass tubes, which are ideal for adding shape to your work. Because of how they are made they have sharp edges, so be careful when using them.

Pearls

Pearls have long been a symbol of beauty and refinement, but the real thing can be quite expensive. However, there are now 'fake' pearls on a crystal base, combining quality at an affordable price with an exciting range of colours.

Hints and tips

....

The beads you use are entirely up to you, so choose them based on your own preference for size, colour and shape, and allow your personal style to dictate what you make. However, if the project is size-dependent, then follow the guidance given by the designer to ensure the finished piece works.

Rivoli crystals

Shaped beads

Feature beads come in many different shapes, such as daggers, drops, cubes and discs, and can be used to add texture and interest to your work. When choosing them, pay attention to how the holes lie.

Dagger beads

Crystal rivolis

These round, pointed-back crystals come in various sizes and are ideal for adding extra sparkle and colour to your work. The crystals are bezelled to hold them tight and these sparkly components can then be added to beadwork.

Cube beads

Drop beads

TOOLS AND MATERIALS

Once you have gathered all the beads required for a project, the next step is getting hold of all the essential tools and other materials which will enable you to create the perfect piece of jewellery.

Fabric cord

Head pins

These lengths of metal have a flat base to stop beads from falling off the end (they look a little like hardware nails). If you find that the beads fall off because the flat end is too small, then thread on a small seed bead first.

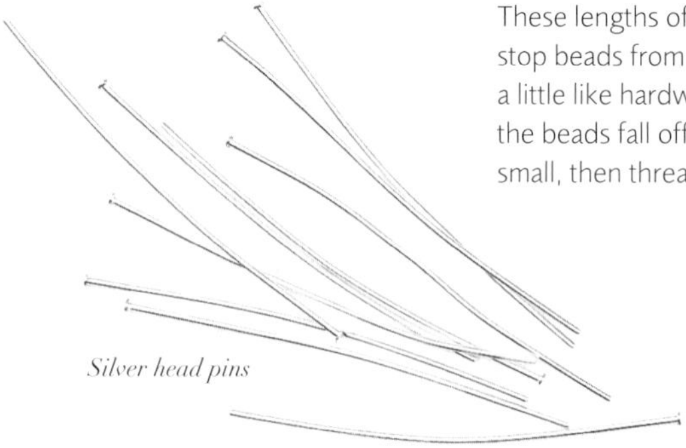

Silver head pins

Needles

Beading needles, available in different lengths and thicknesses, are very fine with small eyes to ensure you can weave through the beads more than once. Choose needles to suit the beads you are using.

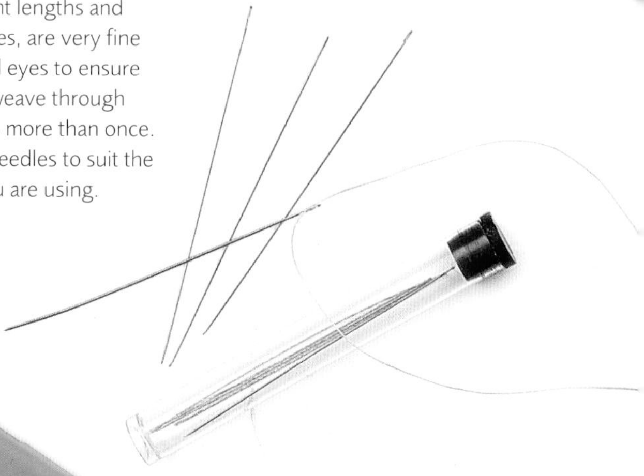

Various threads

Thread

With a wide variety of threads available, which one you use is up to you. It is an important part of your work and relatively inexpensive, so choose carefully and never use thread past its best.

Scissors

Essential for cutting thread, you won't get far in beading without a pair of these! Choose a sharp, pointy pair to help you get into tight spaces and remove thread ends neatly and precisely.

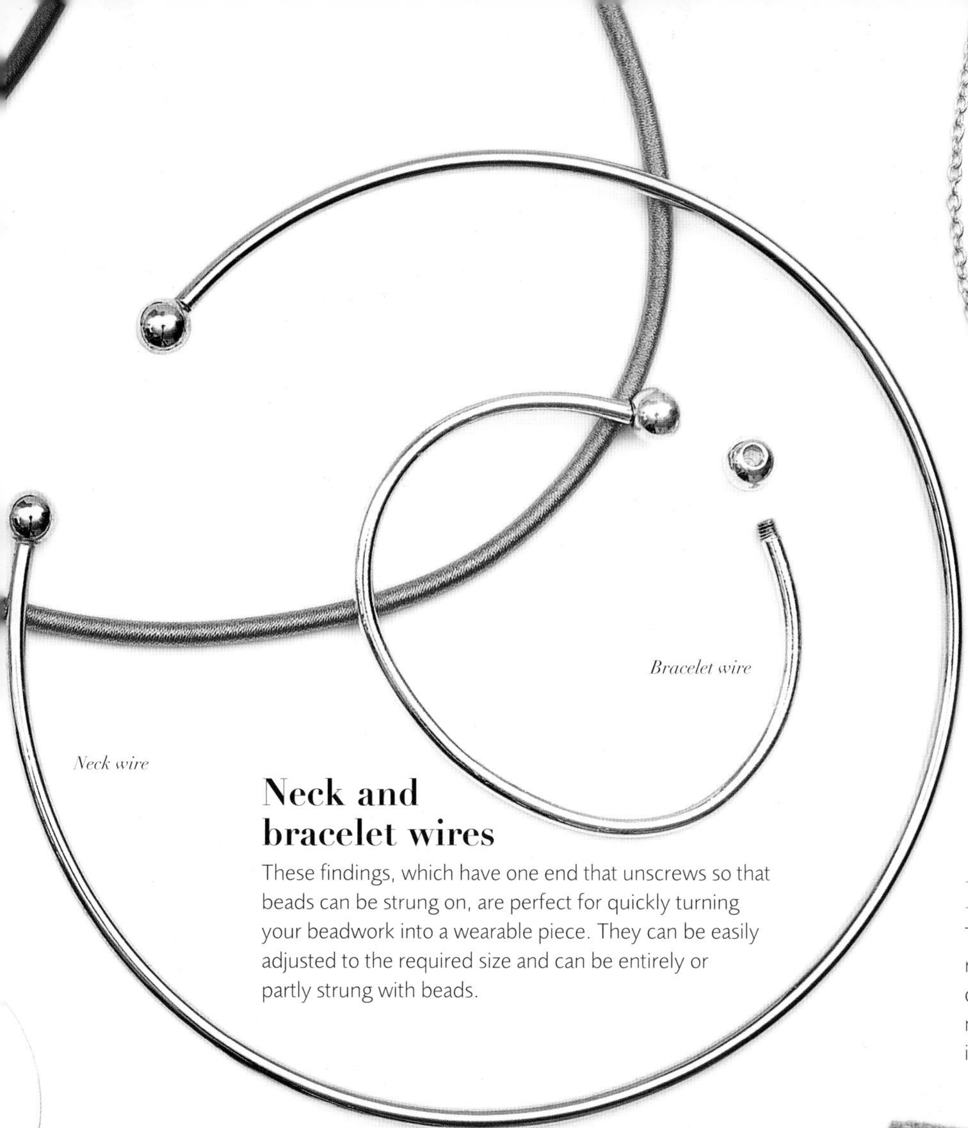

Necklace chains, wide to narrow links

Bracelet wire

Neck wire

Neck and bracelet wires

These findings, which have one end that unscrews so that beads can be strung on, are perfect for quickly turning your beadwork into a wearable piece. They can be easily adjusted to the required size and can be entirely or partly strung with beads.

Bead mat

The ideal beading surface will stop your beads from rolling around and have no loops on the surface to catch on your needle as you pick up beads. Bead mats, designed especially for this purpose, are inexpensive to buy and are perfect for the role.

Clasps

Clasps are essential findings, and whichever ones you opt for comes down to personal preference. Whether you choose a magnetic, fold-over, lobster or toggle clasp, the main things to bear in mind are security and ease of fastening and unfastening.

Selection of lobster and toggle clasps

Whatever project you want to bead, there are some principles and techniques that always remain the same.

Adding and finishing threads

There are many ways to add and finish threads, and you will soon find what works best for you. The basic method is to weave new and old threads securely into your work, making sure they cross over themselves and are held tight. In this diagram, the black thread is the old one, and the red thread is the new one being woven in, ready to continue.

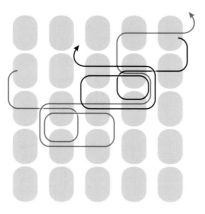

Circling through and going back through

Each of these phrases means something different, and understanding them will help you to correctly follow a pattern or set of instructions.

CIRCLE THROUGH

This means to thread through a bead in the *same direction* you previously threaded through it.

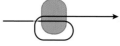

GO BACK THROUGH

This means to thread back through a bead in the *opposite direction* you previously threaded through it.

Adding a stop bead

You can add a stop bead to the thread at the start of your work to help with tension and also to stop the beads you'll add from falling off the thread. Simply pick up a bead, position it where needed and circle through it a few times, ensuring you don't split the thread. Make sure you thread through it enough times so that it doesn't slide off, but not so many that it will be hard to remove later on.

Direction of work?

Which direction you bead is entirely up to you, so experiment to find what works best for you. Some people prefer to work towards themselves and others away from themselves, whereas some mix it up as they go. You may find you always prefer working to the right or the left, so when beading flat work you can turn it over at the end of every row to do this.

Stretching the thread

You may find that when the thread comes off the reel it will be coiled and twisty, making it much more likely to tangle and get knotted. The cure for this is to stretch it. Pull the thread with your hands with sufficient force to straighten it – you'll find it a lot easier to work with. No matter what thread you choose to use, always stretch it – even if it doesn't look twisty – to avoid your work becoming loose later on.

Using a workable length of thread

Every beader has their own idea of what is a workable length of thread; some prefer a longer thread, while others prefer a short thread. An ideal length to start with is double your arm span, which is the distance from the tip of your index finger to your armpit. Try this length and then see if you're happy with it or would prefer a shorter or longer length. Do bear in mind you'll need to leave a tail of thread at the start of your work to finish it later. Never use too long a thread as it will tangle and knot, and you'll bead a lot more slowly and lose the tension – as well as being unnecessary extra work for your arm!

Adding a clasp

There are many different types of clasps and each one may need to be added a different way. When adding a clasp, the aim is to fix it securely and close to your work, and to ensure the thread won't rub against it and fray.

COVERING THE THREAD WITH BEADS
You can use seed beads – size 15 if they fit better – to cover the thread so that it doesn't rub against the clasp and wear away, as it goes through the hole in the clasp.

USING GIMP
Gimp, or French wire, is designed for covering threads when attaching a clasp. It resembles a small spring, but beware – there is no spring to it and it is very fragile. It's best cut with sharp scissors and handled carefully.

Zipping up

'Zipping up' is the term used for joining edges together by replicating the stitching you are beading, usually without adding any new beads. In peyote stitch, this means threading through the beads already there; in brick stitch, it means looping around threads you have already looped around.

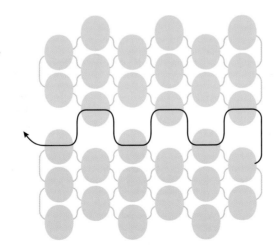

Zipping up in peyote stitch

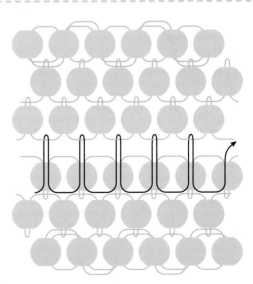

Zipping up in brick stitch

The following pages explain the techniques needed to complete 30 beautiful projects and inspirational variations. Choose your favourite pieces and learn the beading stitches to complete them. The projects are arranged in order of ability, so if you're new to beading, why not start by making a ring or a simple pendant? For those with a little more experience, dive in and choose from a selection of challenging and exciting projects.

Projects

Peyote stitch

TECHNIQUES

Peyote stitch is one of the most common and versatile stitches used in beading. Although it can seem tricky at first, the stitch is based on a simple pattern of making spaces in your work and then filling those spaces with beads.

Hints and tips

You may find it useful to add a stop bead at the start of your work. See p.22 for more details.

Those new to the technique should use alternate bead colours to make it clearer which beads to thread through. Then as you bead each row you will only pick up beads of one colour and go through beads of the other.

When you begin you may find that your work is twisting and it's hard to tell which beads are in row 1 and which are in row 3. Keeping a tight tension on your work will help, but so long as you're not following a complicated colour chart it doesn't matter.

See pp.38–41 for this project.

Even-count peyote stitch

Peyote can be tubular, circular or even spiralled, but flat even-count is the best variation to begin with as all the others are based on this.

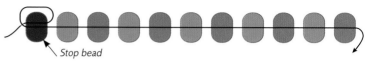

Stop bead

1 Add a stop bead. Pick up an even number of beads (the number of beads you pick up will determine the width of your work). These beads will form the first two rows of peyote stitch.

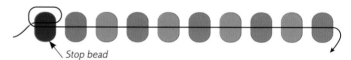

4 Continue adding beads in exactly the same way all along the row. The total number of beads you add will be half the amount you picked up in Step 1.

Odd-count peyote stitch

This is beaded in almost the same way as even-count but it has a figure-eight turn at the end of every other row.

Stop bead

1 Add a stop bead. Pick up an odd number of beads (just as with even-count peyote the number of beads you pick up will determine the width of your work; these beads will form the first two rows).

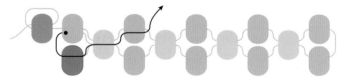

4 Pick up one new bead (the last bead in row 3). Thread through the second bead in from the edge of your work (the last bead in row 2) and the lowest bead of the next pair (second to last bead of row 1). The third row is now finished.

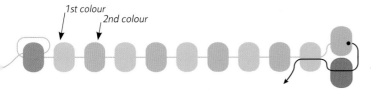

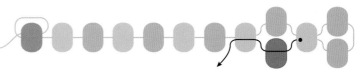

2 To bead row 3, pick up one bead (if using two colours then pick up one in the second colour). Missing the last bead added in Step 1, take the needle and thread back through the next bead along.

3 Pick up one more bead (again in the second colour), and missing the next bead added in Step 1, thread through the next one along. You are now threading through the beads that will make up row 2 and ignoring those that will form row 1.

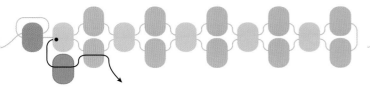

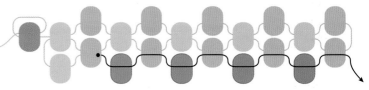

5 You are now changing direction again to begin beading the fourth row. Pick up one new bead (in the first colour) and thread through the last bead you added in the previous row.

6 Repeat adding single beads (of the first colour) all along the row until you have filled all the spaces. Then change direction and continue in this manner until your work is as long as desired.

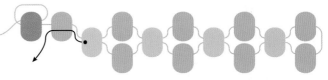

2 Using regular peyote stitch, bead all the way along the row until you can't easily add another bead.

3 You now need to turn so you can fill in the missing bead and be in a position to continue. Without picking up a new bead, thread down through the next bead along that sits in the first row (the first bead you picked up).

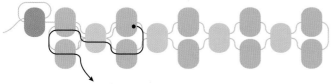

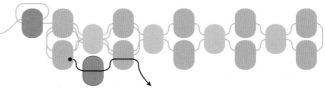

5 Thread through the bead above the one you are currently exiting (pointing back towards the end of the row). Thread through the next two beads along to reach the edge and then thread back through the last new bead added (pointing towards the body of the piece).

6 Continue beading using regular peyote stitch, remembering that you only have to perform this turn at the end of every other row.

Unite the old and the new with this embellished vintage key.

Skeleton key

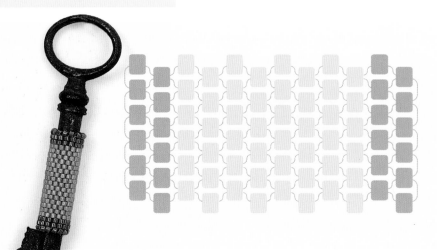

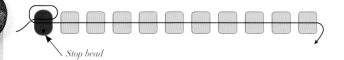

Stop bead

1 Using a comfortable length of thread, pick up as many beads as the length you would like to make your embellishment. You can use either odd- or even-count peyote, depending on how many beads you pick up.

TOOLS AND MATERIALS

★ Thread
★ Scissors
★ Beading needle
★ 1–2g size 11 cylinder beads
★ Vintage key

TECHNIQUE

Peyote stitch (see pp.26–27)

SIZE

Dependent on key size

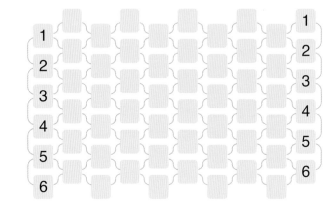

2 Using peyote stitch, bead an even number of rows until your work is wide enough to fold around the key shank. You can tell when you have an even number of rows as you will have the same number of edge beads on each side.

Here, the blue beads are threaded on at the beginning and end, with the pink beads in between. The ends are then adorned with extra beads in the same way as Step 5 of the Polka Dot Delight pendant (see p.58).

Embellishing a vintage key makes it unique and helps you to put your own stamp on it. There are lots of different patterns you could bead into your work, so why not experiment to see what you can achieve?

3 Place the key shank along the length of the piece. Bring the start and end edges of your work together and 'zip' them together by weaving from one side to the other, joining the piece into a tube. Weave back and forth a couple of times to secure.

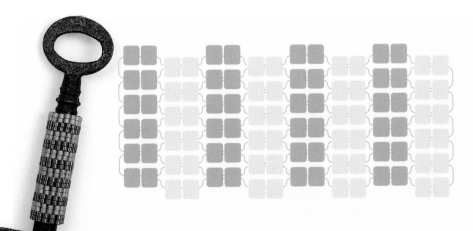

This striped variation uses two different bead colours and two-drop peyote for a different look.

Hints and tips

The finished keys can be hung from chains or cords of your choice, or even used as ornaments.

This bold bangle is made using dagger beads to create added interest and texture. If it's too spiky for your taste, make it with smaller drop beads.

DESIGNER: Arantxa A.

Dagger bangle

Stop bead

1 Using a comfortable length of thread, slide a stop bead onto the thread and then circle through the same bead again, leaving a 12.5 cm (5 in) tail. This bead won't be part of your work and will be removed later.

2 Pick up an even number of A beads – enough so that when the beaded length is formed into a loop it will slide over your hand. To help with sizing, 96 beads will make a small bangle, 102 a medium bangle and 110 a large bangle.

3 Thread through the first bead to join the ends together and form the base circle.

4 Pick up one A bead and, skipping the next bead in the base circle, thread through the next to make a single peyote stitch.

TOOLS AND MATERIALS

★ Beading thread
★ Scissors
★ Beading needle
★ 11–13g size 8 seed beads (A beads)
★ 3g size 11 seed beads (B beads)

For small bangle (16 cm/6¼ in inner circumference)
336 dagger beads size 3/10 mm

For medium bangle (18 cm/7 in inner circumference)
357 dagger beads size 3/10 mm

For large bangle (19 cm/7½ in inner circumference)
385 dagger beads size 3/10 mm

TECHNIQUE

Peyote stitch (see pp.26–27)

SIZE

See Tools and Materials

PROJECT COLOURWAY

In this project, the seed beads peek out between the daggers, so the colour of the seed beads you use will show. You can use complementary colours for a seamless look or clashing colours for a statement piece.

Gold seed beads combine with copper-gold daggers for a warm colour combination.

continued overleaf ▶

Dagger beads add lots of texture and interest to these bangles. The seed beads you use will show, so you can decide whether to use a complementary colour or a contrasting one to alter the look of your piece.

5 Repeat Step 4 to add single beads all around the base circle. The number of beads you add will be half the number you originally picked up in Step 2.

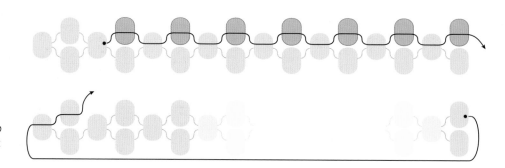

6 At the end of the round, step up so that you exit through the first bead added in Step 4.

7 You now have three rounds of peyote stitch (the beads in the base circle count as two rounds). Repeat adding single beads for six more rounds so that you have a total of nine rounds.

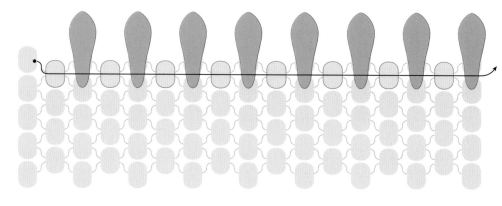

8 Begin adding the dagger beads. Note that you will start on the second round of peyote stitch, leaving the first one free of embellishment. Weave through a seed bead in the second round, pick up a dagger bead and pass through the next bead of this round. Continue adding dagger beads all around the round.

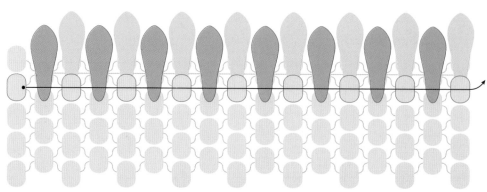

9 Weave to exit an A bead in the next round of peyote stitch and add a second round of dagger beads in the same way you added the first.

10 Repeat Step 9 five more times until you have added a total of seven rounds of dagger beads.

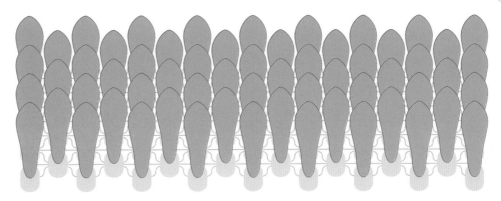

11 While you have been adding the dagger beads, the edges of the original peyote stitch will have curved inwards. The edges will now resemble this illustration.

12 Using B beads, bead inside the bangle to bring the edges of the beadwork together. Weave to exit an A bead in either of the edge rounds and, using B beads, add a round of peyote stitch.

13 Using B beads, add four more rounds of peyote stitch. Weave to join the last round of B beads to the other edge round of A beads. Weave all around your work to ensure the edges are united fully, then weave the threads in to secure, removing the stop bead as you go.

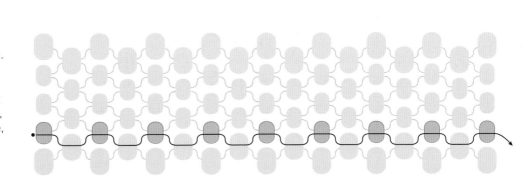

This spiral bracelet is a fun and funky variation of peyote stitch, and lets you go wild with your beads!

Cellini spiral bracelet

TOOLS AND MATERIALS
★ Beading thread
★ Scissors
★ Beading needle
★ 10g size 11 seed beads in main colour (A beads)
★ 15g size 8 seed beads in main colour (B beads)
★ 25g size 6 seed beads in main colour (C beads)
★ 15g size 6 seed beads in highlight colour (D beads)

TECHNIQUE
Peyote stitch (see pp.26–27)

SIZE
2 cm (¾ in) wide

PROJECT COLOURWAY
Blue and orange are complementary colours, and this scheme stretches that to pair navy blue and mustard yellow to dramatic effect. Using only a dash of yellow prevents the colours from fighting each other.

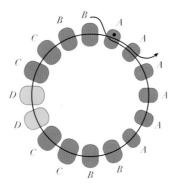

1 Add a stop bead if desired (see p.22) and pick beads in this order: six A beads, two B, two C, two D, two C and two B beads. Thread through two A beads to join into the base circle.

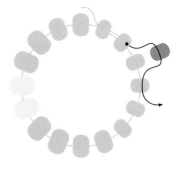

2 You will now bead all around the base circle using peyote stitch. Pick up one A bead, skip one A bead in the base circle and thread into the next one.

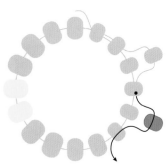

3 Pick up one A bead, skip one A bead in the base circle and thread into the next A bead.

4 Pick up one A bead, skip one B bead in the base circle and thread into the next B bead.

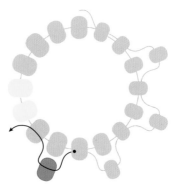

5 Pick up one B bead, skip one C bead in the base circle and thread into the next C bead.

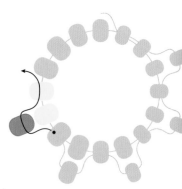

6 Pick up one C bead, skip one D bead in the base circle and thread into the next D bead.

continued overleaf ▶

Cellini spiral is a lot easier to bead than it looks. It is simply the combination of beads you use that do all of the visual work. This version plays up the spiral detail of the stitch by using one bead of a different colour.

Hints and tips

Your work won't look right for a few rounds, but bear with it and soon all the different-size beads will fall into place.

If you ever get lost, you just need to remember to pick up the same bead as the one you are exiting.

Joining the ends together may seem confusing, but go slow and remember it is just the same as what you have already beaded, but instead of picking up a new bead for each stitch, you're using one that is already there.

MORE COLOURWAYS

Natural shades always produce a soft, subtle colour scheme. Avocado green and golden brown are a warm combination that pair well and bring out the best in each other.

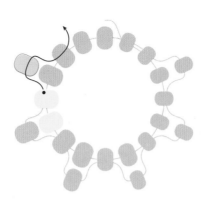

7 Pick up one D bead, skip one C bead in the base circle and thread into the next C bead.

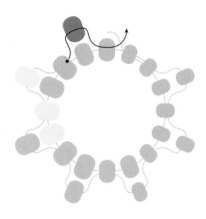

8 Pick up one C bead, skip one B bead in the base circle and thread into the next B bead.

Using only the equivalents of A and B beads, and picking up eight A and two B beads for the base circle, the smaller contrast in bead sizes shows that Cellini spiral can also be subtle.

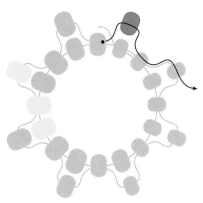

9 Pick up one B bead, skip one A bead in the base circle and thread into the next A bead. This is the end of the round, so you need to step up to exit the first A bead added in this round to finish.

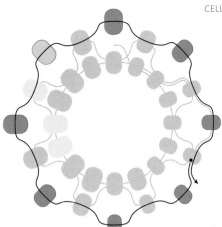

10 Continue beading peyote stitch, ensuring that you pick up the same bead as the one you are exiting and thread into the next bead along. Pull tight as you work and what you create will turn into a tube.

11 When your beadwork is long enough to fit around your wrist, bring the ends together and rotate each end until the beadwork matches up.

Before zipping the ends of your work, make sure to rotate both ends so that they match exactly.

12 Weave from one end of the work into the other, ensuring that the bead you thread through is the same as the one you are exiting. Weave all around, joining the two ends securely.

Get medalling for an adaptable and interchangeable necklace that should have you winning awards!

Rivoli medals necklace

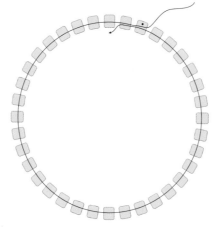

TOOLS AND MATERIALS

★ Thread
★ Scissors
★ Beading needle
★ 25g size 11 cylinder beads (A beads)
★ 2g size 15 seed beads (B beads)
★ Neck wire with screw-on ball ends
★ 25 x 14 mm round crystal rivolis

TECHNIQUE

Peyote stitch (see pp.26–27)

SIZE

2 cm (¾ in) across

PROJECT COLOURWAY

Silver cylinder beads act as the perfect neutral to help combine all the colours of the rainbow and beyond in this necklace. The metal-coated beads also make this piece look as though it was made by a silversmith.

1 Using a long length of thread, pick up 36 A beads. Circle through the first two beads and leave a long tail. You will return to this tail later.

2 Using peyote stitch, add a round with one A bead in every space. At the end you will need to make sure you step up to exit the first bead added.

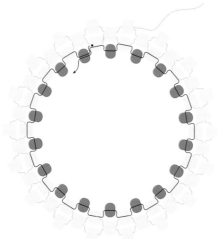

3 Using peyote stitch, add a round with one B bead in every space. At the end you will need to make sure you step up to exit the first bead added. Pull tight as you work and ensure that these new beads sit inside the circle already made.

4 Using peyote stitch, add a round with one B bead in every space. At the end you will need to make sure you step up to exit the first bead added. Weave this end of the thread into your work to secure, then trim. Continue pulling tight, as it is the decrease in bead size and the tension that will hold the crystal in place.

continued overleaf ▶

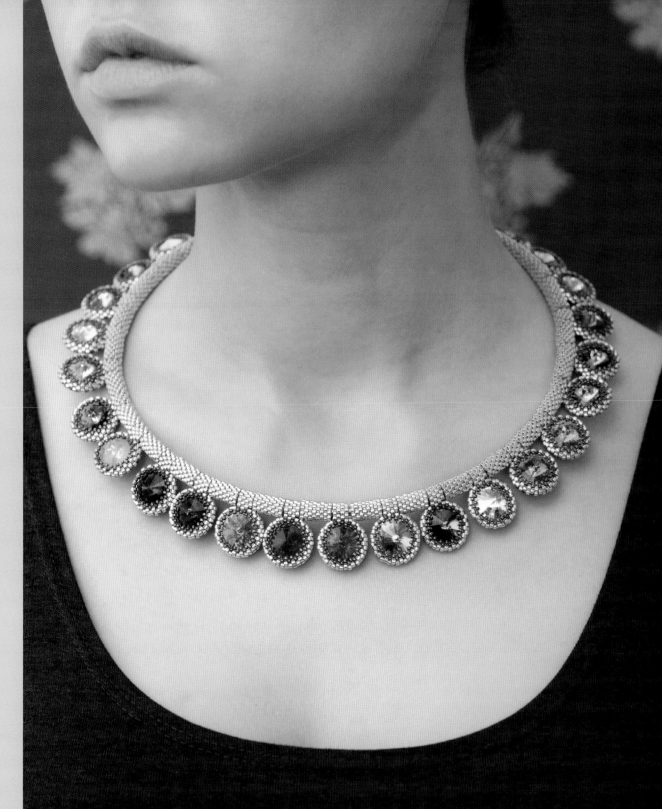

This dramatic necklace lets you run wild with colour. Remember that as soon as you've made one medal, you can wear it on your neck wire.

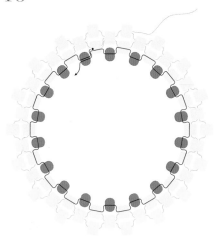

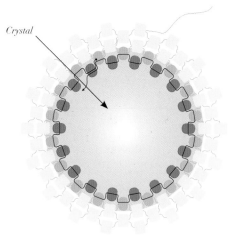

Crystal

5 Return to the tail thread from Step 1 and, using peyote stitch, add a round with one B bead in every space. At the end you will need to make sure you step up to exit the first bead added. Pull tight as you work and ensure that these new beads sit inside the circle you have already made.

6 Place one of the crystals into your work so that its front faces out through the beads added in Steps 3 and 4. Continuing at the back of your work and using peyote stitch, add one more round with one B bead in every space holding the crystal in place.

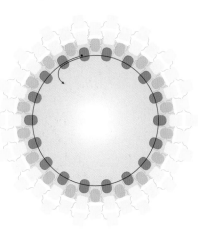

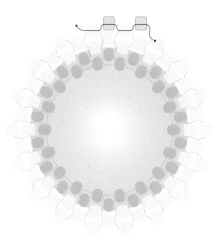

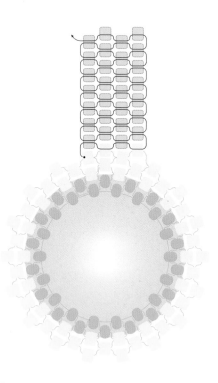

7 If you are concerned about holding the crystal in place, you can weave through the beads added in Step 6 without adding any new beads. The weaving will sit at the back of your work, so don't worry about it showing.

8 Weave to exit any bead in either of the two outer rounds of A beads. Pick up one A bead and thread into the next A bead on the same round as the one you exited. Pick up one A bead and thread into the next A bead on the same round as the one you exited.

9 Change direction and, using peyote stitch, add one A bead into each of the two spaces created by the new beads added in Step 8. Continue changing direction and adding rows using just two beads until you have added a total of 15 rows using 30 beads. If your chosen neck wire is quite thick, then you can add more rows of beads, so long as it is an odd number of rows.

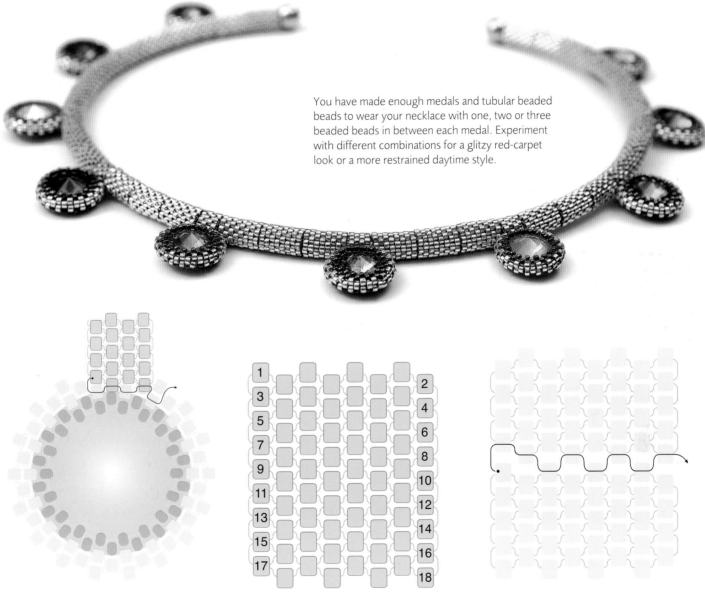

You have made enough medals and tubular beaded beads to wear your necklace with one, two or three beaded beads in between each medal. Experiment with different combinations for a glitzy red-carpet look or a more restrained daytime style.

10 Fold this new strip of beadwork so its edge beads connect with the appropriate A beads in the other outside round of A beads, and 'zip' the new beads to this round (see p.23). Repeat Steps 1–10 to bezel all the crystals.

11 To make the tubular beaded beads, begin with eight A beads and bead a strip of beadwork 18 rows long. To know when you've reached 18 rows, simply count the number of beads along the edges and add the two amounts together for the total number of rows.

12 Bring the beginning and ending edges together and zip your work into a tube by mimicking peyote stitch but using the beads already there rather than adding new ones. Repeat Steps 11 and 12 to make 30 tubular beaded beads.

With a two-drop peyote stitch base, this ring has lots of scope for embellishment and variation. It is also ideal for using up small quantities of beads.

SKILL LEVEL: INTERMEDIATE

Fireworks ring

TOOLS AND MATERIALS
★ Beading thread
★ Scissors
★ Beading needle
★ 2–3g size 11 cylinder or seed beads (for the ring base and fringe)
★ Sprinkle of cylinder or seed beads (for the fringe ends)

TECHNIQUE
Peyote stitch (see pp.26–27)

SIZE
1.2 cm (½ in) wide

PROJECT COLOURWAY
Lime green is the perfect backdrop for an injection of colour! These rings add in dots of gold, bronze, pink and blue for extra contrast and to ensure that they really stand out.

Stop bead

1 Add a stop bead if desired (see p.22) and pick up eight base beads. Change direction, pick up two more base beads and, skipping the last two, take the needle and thread through the next two base beads. This is two-drop peyote stitch.

2 Pick up two more base beads and thread through the next two on the base.

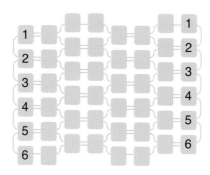

3 Continue beading two-drop peyote stitch until you have added enough rows to fit around your finger. You need an even number of rows to ensure the ends will join correctly.

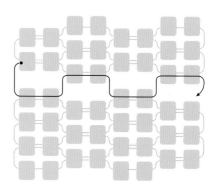

4 Bring the ends of your beadwork together and weave from side to side to join the ends into a ring.

5 Weave to exit any of the base beads. Pick up between two and 15 base beads and one fringe end bead.

Hints and tips
· · · · · · · · · · · · · · ·
You can use single-drop peyote stitch to make this ring, or even brick stitch if desired.
· ·
If you want an extra touch of bling, why not use a small crystal as the second-to-last bead in the fringes?
· ·
Keep the fringes you add to one area so that they don't fall between your fingers.

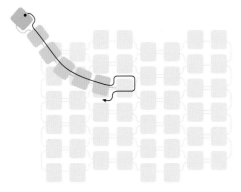

6 Skipping the last bead added, thread through the other beads and back into the same base bead, but in the opposite direction to which you exited it. This ensures that the fringe sits evenly on top of the base.

7 Weave to exit a new base bead and continue adding fringes until you have added as many as desired. You can keep all the fringes the same or you can make some longer or shorter, and even add different coloured end beads, too.

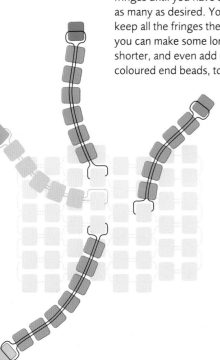

The simple beaded base of this ring is perfect for adding extra embellishment. If you use cylinder beads, their large holes will mean you can weave through them lots of times and really go wild with the extra touches.

Ladder stitch

TECHNIQUES

Ladder stitch is not only a stitch in its own right but also the base for two common beading stitches: brick stitch and herringbone stitch.

Hints and tips

Pay attention to the basic pattern to ensure your work doesn't get twisted and you don't enter and exit beads in the wrong direction.

Look out for the simple circular path – it will help you to learn the stitch.

In ladder stitch, the individual beads (or group of beads in two- or more drop) are called 'rungs'.

See pp.46–49 for this project.

Basic ladder stitch

When beading this stitch you need to pay attention to the direction the needle exits and enters each bead added.

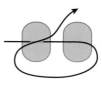

1 Using a comfortable length of thread, pick up two beads and circle through the first one again (remember that circle through means to go through in the same direction as before).

2 Pull on the thread so that the beads lie neatly next to each other.

3 Circle through the second bead to bring yourself into the correct position to continue beading.

4 Pick up one new bead. Circle through the previous bead to join the new bead to it.

5 Circle through the new bead to be in the correct position to continue.

6 Repeat Steps 4 and 5 to continue adding new beads until your work is the length you require. Note that if you exit a bead from the top, you will go into the next bead from the top, and vice versa.

Two-drop and more

Ladder stitch can be beaded with two or more beads, replacing just one bead for a different look and taller beadwork. You simply treat the groups of beads as though they were singular.

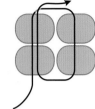 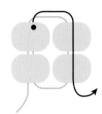 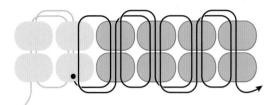

1 For two-drop ladder stitch pick up four beads to begin. Circle through the first two to join them together.

2 Circle through the second two to get into position to continue.

3 Continue to bead as for regular ladder stitch but using two (or more) beads in place of single beads.

Joining the ends

Ladder stitch can be made continual (into a loop, circle or band) by joining the ends together.

Bring the start and end of your work together.

1 Once your work is as long as you require, bring the first and last beads together.

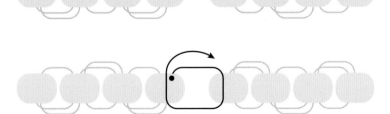

2 Circle through the first bead as though it was a new bead and circle through the last bead again.

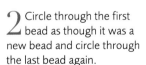

3 Circle through the first bead again to secure.

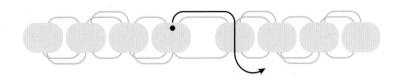 

Bugle beads
lend themselves
perfectly to ladder
stitch and especially
this project.

Linked ladders bracelet

1 Using a long length of thread and leaving a long enough tail (which you will use to later add the clasp), pick up two bugle beads. Circle through the first bead to join them together.

2 Circle through the second bugle bead and then the first one again to reposition yourself to continue. This circling through is to ensure the tail thread is pointing the right way so that you can use it to attach the clasp later.

3 Pick up one more bugle bead and ladder stitch it to the bead you are exiting by circling through it and then the new bead.

TOOLS AND MATERIALS

★ Thread
★ Scissors
★ Beading needle
★ 5g 12 mm twisted bugle beads
★ Clasp

TECHNIQUE

Ladder stitch (see pp.44–45)

SIZE

1.5 cm (5/8 in) wide, 20 cm (8 in) long

PROJECT COLOURWAY

Dark, grass, lime and mid-green all combine in this monochromatic colour scheme. If you are ever stuck for a colour scheme, then remember that using different shades of one colour always creates a winning result.

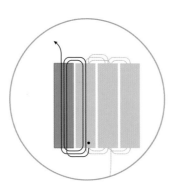

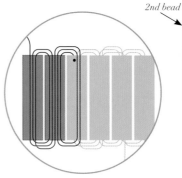

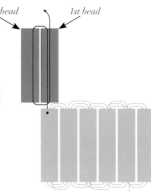

2nd bead   1st bead

5 Pick up one more bugle bead and ladder stitch it to the bead you are exiting by circling through it and then the new bead. Rethread through the same path to secure.

6 Repeat adding new beads and retracing the path until you have six beads ladder-stitched together. Make sure the beads sit neatly beside each other before moving on to a new step.

7 To begin the second motif, pick up two bugle beads and slide them close to the work already beaded. Circle through the first new bead to connect them together.

continued overleaf ▶

4 In order to keep the beads nice and tight together, from now on you must always rethread through each bead once more and keep a tight tension.

Make sure you bring the beginning of the second motif tight to the first before you continue.

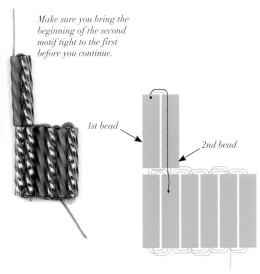

1st bead

2nd bead

8 Circle through the second new bead added to ladder stitch them together so that you are in the correct position to continue. Exiting the second new bead added, turn these two beads so that they both sit on top of the first motif. Note that the first and second beads of the second motif have now swapped places. This is correct and will happen as you bead each new motif.

The green bracelet uses twisted bugles for an extra touch of texture.

The top bracelet here is a version of the green one at the bottom, but beaded in shades of brown, beige and gold. The centre variation uses smaller bugle beads and only four per motif for a more delicate look.

Hints and tips

You can use fewer or more bugles for each motif if desired – or even use multiple seed beads instead of bugles.

MORE COLOURWAYS

The finish of a bead is a way to add contrast when the colour scheme is muted. Here, golds, beiges and browns combine for a warm combination, but the colours are stopped from visually running into one another by the use of both matt and shiny finishes.

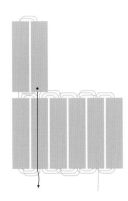

9 Thread from the bead you are exiting into the fifth bead of the first motif. You may find that you have to adjust your work so that the beads sit closely together and the motifs are joined. This needs to be done before you continue, as it is harder to fix later on.

10 Circle through the sixth bead in the first motif and into what is now the second bead in the second motif. Circle all the way through the two beads that sit at the end of the first motif and the two at the start of the second to secure them closely together.

11 Using ladder stitch and repeating Steps 3 and 4, add four new beads to the second motif for a total of six. You don't have to have six beads in each motif – the number you use is entirely up to you.

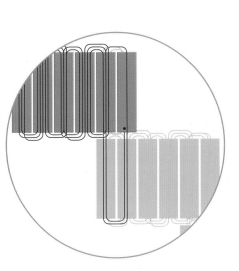

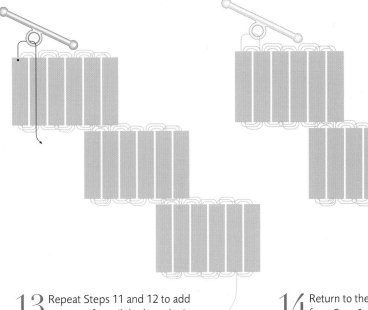

12 Repeat Steps 7–10 to begin beading a new motif (the third), remembering that the first and second beads swap places. This is especially important to know if you are using a specific colour pattern.

13 Repeat Steps 11 and 12 to add new motifs until the bracelet is the length you require. Don't forget to allow for the clasp, so don't make the bracelet too long. Using the remaining thread to attach the end of the bracelet securely to one half of the clasp.

14 Return to the tail thread from Step 1 and use it to attach the other half of the clasp to the start of your work.

Taking ladder stitch three-dimensional leads to exciting jewellery.

Spiked ladders bangle

TOOLS AND MATERIALS
★ Thread
★ Scissors
★ Beading needle
★ 20g 9 mm bugle beads

TECHNIQUE
Ladder stitch (see pp.44–45)

SIZE
1 cm (3/8 in) wide, 8 mm (1/3 in) high

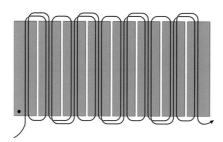

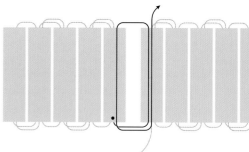

1 Using a long length of thread, bead a strip of ladder stitch long enough to fit comfortably around your wrist. Make sure the beaded strip is a multiple of four to ensure the pattern will work (note that the diagrams show the beadwork shorter than yours will be).

2 Bring the ends of the strip together and join the beads (see Zipping up on p.23). If you're not sure about the sizing at this stage you can leave the joining until later. These beads form the base.

3 From now on, the diagrams show your work from the edge so that you can see how the beads are joined to one another. Exit one of the beads and ladder stitch a new bead onto it, then ladder stitch this new bead to the next one along in the base. From now, as you add new beads, you will weave through the same thread path multiple times to hold all the beads very tightly together.

Hints and tips

As the thread shows a lot in the work, choose one that coordinates closely or contrasts for a different look.

Bugle beads have sharp edges, so work slowly and be careful when pulling the thread tight around the edges of the bead holes.

Multiple weaving not only holds the beads together for a neater look and shape to the bangle, but also means the beads don't move around, reducing the chances of them cutting through the thread.

4 Ladder stitch a new bead to the one added in Step 3 and then stitch it to the second bead in the base and also the next one along. As you work, each new bead needs to be stitched multiple times to the beads touching it.

continued overleaf ▶

This dramatic bangle
with its geometric
shaping looks great from
all angles. Why not make
an armful to create a
really powerful effect?

5 Continue adding beads until you have covered every space in the base. These new beads form the top base.

6 Exiting a bead in the top base, stitch a new bead to it and then to the bead next to where you exited.

7 Stitch a new bead to the last new one added, the second one the last new bead was stitched to, and then to the next bead along in the top base.

8 Add another bead so that you have three on top of the top base, making sure every bead is stitched multiple times to all those it touches.

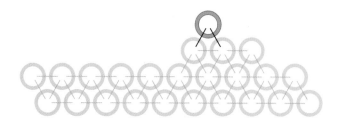

9 Stitch a new bead to the last of the three just added, then join this bead to the second of the new beads just added.

10 Stitch a new bead to the last one added and to the two beads that sit directly under it.

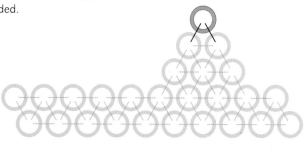

11 Stitch a new bead to the last one just added and to the two beads that sit directly underneath it.

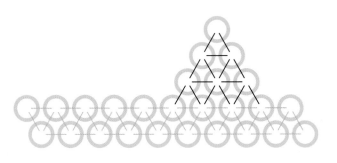

12 Weave through the six beads added to the top base, ensuring that no thread paths are left unwoven.

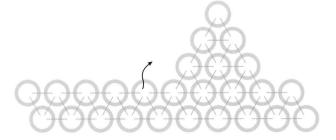

13 Weave down to the next bead in the top base, which has no other beads added on top of it.

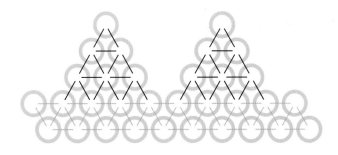

14 Repeat Steps 6–13, adding 'spikes' formed of six new beads until the whole of the top base is covered.

If you're unsure about sizing, skip joining in Step 2 and instead join once all the spikes are beaded.

Brick stitch

TECHNIQUES

Brick stitch is named for the way the beads resemble bricks in a wall. This stitch is ideal for beginners, as it is easy to see where each bead goes.

Hints and tips

Make sure you firmly catch the threads you are attaching your beads to by looping around the previous thread, catching it with the needle and thread.

Picking up two beads at the start of a row ensures the thread doesn't show.

Which method you choose for starting or ending a row is up to you – it will vary from project to project.

See pp.62–63 for this project.

Basic brick stitch

Brick stitch grows from a ladder stitch base, with each subsequent row joined to the previous one bead by bead. The join is made using the loops of thread which join the beads in the previous row.

1 Begin with a ladder stitch base the width you desire (see pp.44–45). Pick up two seed beads and slide them towards your work. Take the needle and thread under the loop of thread linking the first and second beads in the ladder.

2 Take the needle and thread back through the second bead just picked up and pull tight.

Different starts and ends

Brick stitch can have a different start and end to each row, depending on the shape you want to create.

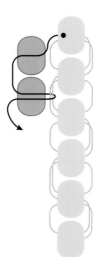

1 For an 'in-bead' start, simply link the first two beads of a row to the loop of thread separating the second and third beads of the previous row. You can then secure the beads as you did for the 'out-bead' start (see Step 3, above right), making sure to link around the correct loop.

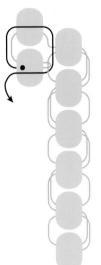

3 This is an 'out-bead' start and you can now secure the beads by threading up the first bead, linking around the same thread loop, and then back down the second bead.

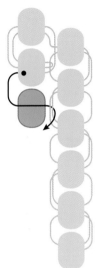

4 Pick up a new bead and slide it onto your work. Take the needle and thread under the next thread loop in the ladder stitch base. Pull the thread so that no slack remains.

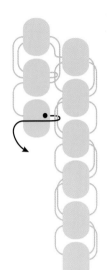

5 Thread back through the bead just added and pull tight so that the bead lies nicely beside the other beads.

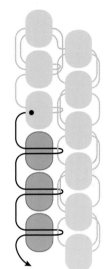

6 Repeat Steps 4 and 5 to continue beading along the row. Stop when you have added a single bead to the last thread loop.

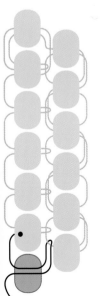

2 For an 'out-bead' end, brick stitch one more bead to the last loop of thread at the end of a row. You will need to secure these last two beads together as you do with the beads at the start of a row.

Two-drop and beyond

Just as with ladder stitch, brick stitch can be beaded with more than one bead in each spot.

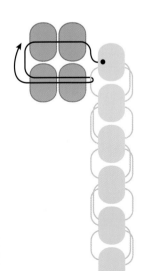

1 Bead your ladder stitch base as wide as desired (it can be in singular or more drops). For two-drop, pick up four beads to begin the brick stitch row. Make sure to treat the pairs of beads as a single one.

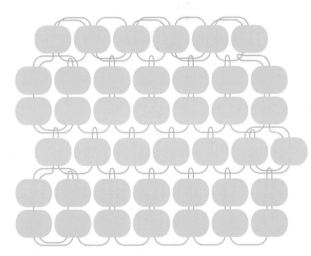

2 Continue beading rows of brick stitch to create your work. You can vary the rows between one or more drops as desired.

Big, bold beads grow fast and give you a colourful bracelet in next to no time.

Sassy stripes bracelet

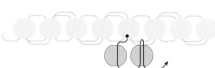

1 Thread the needle with a long piece of thread. Leaving a tail of thread at least 38 cm (15 in), ladder stitch as many beads of a single colour as you need to comfortably fit around your wrist. Join the ends of the ladder stitch together to form a circle.

2 Using brick stitch and a new colour, add a round of beads. To start the round, use an 'out-bead' start, adding two beads at once.

TOOLS AND MATERIALS
★ Beading thread
★ Scissors
★ Beading needle
★ Approximately 40 x 8 mm plastic beads in six colours (I used pink, green, lilac, orange, red and blue)

TECHNIQUES
Ladder stitch (see pp.44–45)
Brick stitch (see pp.54–55)

SIZE
5.5 cm (2¼ in) wide

3 To finish each round, thread down the first bead picked up, loop around the appropriate thread loop, and thread back through the same bead. This ensures the first and last beads have a thread loop joining them.

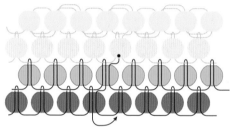

4 Add two more rounds using new colours.

PROJECT COLOURWAY
This colour combination uses stripes of pink, green, lilac, orange, red and blue to dramatic effect. The mixture of colours means this bracelet will go with any outfit and brightens up even the dullest dress.

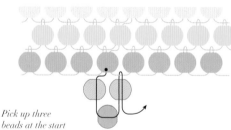

Pick up three beads at the start of the last round to hide the threads.

5 As you add the fifth round, begin by picking up one bead in the colour you want to use for this last stripe, one random-coloured bead and another bead in the colour you want the stripe to be. Thread back through the third bead added.

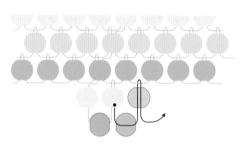

6 For each stitch in the rest of the round, pick up one random-coloured bead and one stripe-coloured bead. Loop around the thread and then pass back through the stripe-coloured bead.

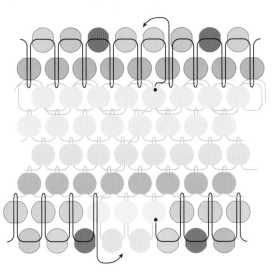

7 To finish the round, pick up one random-
coloured bead and thread through the first bead
picked up in this round. Loop around the thread
and then back down the first bead. Return to the
tail thread and repeat Steps 5–7 at this edge, using
the last colour.

Hints and tips

*This bracelet can be made with additional
or fewer rounds, depending on your
preference.*

*Instead of using round beads as the random
beads in the last rounds, why not try a
different shape?*

*If the holes in your beads are very large you
may want to use a thicker thread, or use
the thread doubled to keep the bracelet from
being too loose or floppy.*

Bold colour, paired with strong stripes,
make this a bracelet no one can ignore!
Instead of horizontal stripes, you can
experiment with different patterns and
stripes (why not try diagonals?) to alter
the look and give you new variations.

Add spots and texture to your beading for a fun and easily adaptable pendant.

Polka dot delight pendant

1 Ladder stitch nine A beads together and join the ends to form a circle. Leave a long tail that you will use to embellish the end later. Your work will now form a tube, but for clarity, the diagrams will show it as flat.

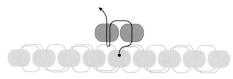

2 Using A beads, begin to brick stitch new beads to the ladder stitch base. It doesn't matter if you use 'in' or 'out' starts.

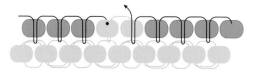

3 Once you have added nine new beads, join the ends together. Do this by threading down the first bead added in Step 2 as though you are adding it as a new bead. Loop around the thread and go back through the bead.

TOOLS AND MATERIALS
★ Thread
★ Scissors
★ Beading needle
★ 12g size 8 seed beads for the base (A beads)
★ 3g size 8 seed beads in a mix of colours (B beads)
★ Neck chain

TECHNIQUES
Ladder stitch (see pp.44–45)
Brick stitch (see pp.54–55)

SIZE
1.5 cm (⁵⁄8 in) wide, 11 cm (4¹⁄4 in) long

PROJECT COLOURWAY
Matt seafoam green is the perfect subtle background colour for this piece. Shiny metallic beads in pink, yellow and orange bring high contrast and extra visual interest.

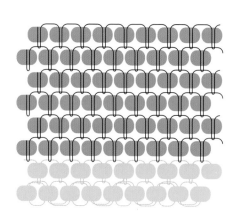

4 Repeat Steps 2 and 3 to add rounds of brick stitch until the pendant is as long as desired. A total of 50 rounds of brick stitch have been beaded here. What you have beaded so far is the base.

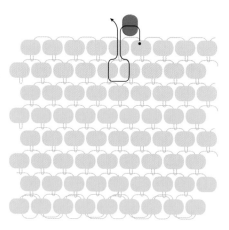

5 To add the embellishments to the ends of your work and to tighten the openings for a neater finish, pick up one A bead. Thread through the next brick-stitched bead in the base and weave through your work to exit this base bead again. The embellishment beads are shown as red in the diagrams.

continued overleaf ▶

Hints
and tips
....
*Using nine beads in the
base gives you the pattern
shown here. If you want to make
the pendant longer or fatter, you
need to remove or add groups
of three beads in Step 1.*

Variations on a theme
give you a matching
pendant and bracelet
that can be mixed and
matched to create the
perfect combination.

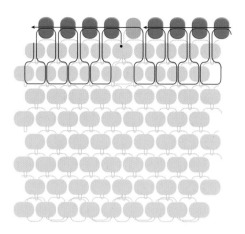

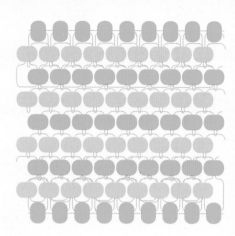

If you want a more delicate pendant, then this smaller variation (see right) is perfect. Simply bead a ladder of six beads and then bead rounds of brick stitch, alternating between A and B beads. Embellish the ends as in the large pendant but using B beads.

6 Repeat Step 5 to add a total of nine new beads to the end of the base. Weave all the way through these new beads a few times to bring them closer together and then return to the tail thread from Step 1 and embellish the other end of the base.

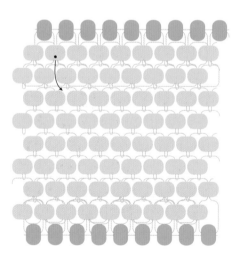

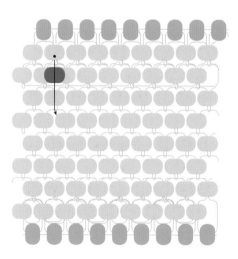

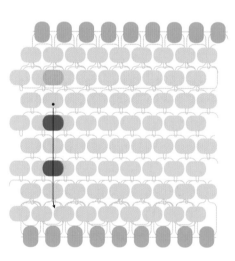

7 Weave so that you are exiting any of the beads in either the ladder stitch round or the last round of brick stitch with the needle facing towards the body of your work, not the edge.

8 Pick up one B bead and weave into the next bead two rounds down from where you exited. The bead you will enter will sit inline with the one you are exiting. For clarity, the B beads are shown in blue in the diagrams.

9 Pick up one B bead and stitch into the bead two rounds below the one you are exiting. Repeat, adding embellishment beads in this way all along the base.

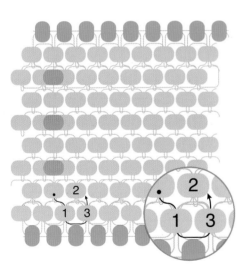

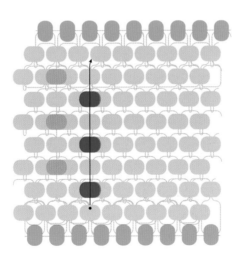

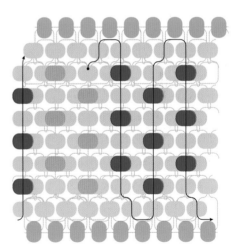

10 The 'stacks' of beads in brick stitch are staggered so that the next one overlaps with the previous one. Weave so that you are exiting the last bead three stacks away from where you did your last embellishment, facing into your work.

11 Pick up one B bead and stitch into the bead two rounds below the one you are exiting. Repeat adding embellishment beads in this way all along the base.

12 Repeat Steps 10 and 11 to add a total of six lengths of embellishment beads to the base. Thread the neck chain through the pendant.

Woohoo to these owls!
Dress up your ears
with a set of cute
feathered friends.
You can make these
in any colour
combination and once
you've mastered the
technique they'll
take no time at all
to make.

TOOLS AND MATERIALS
★ Thread
★ Scissors
★ Beading needle
★ 72 size 11 cylinder beads in red
★ 170 size 11 cylinder beads in black
★ 54 size 11 cylinder beads in silver
★ 24 size 11 cylinder beads in white
★ Pair of silver hoop earrings

TECHNIQUES
Ladder stitch (see pp.44–45)
Brick stitch (see pp.54–55)

SIZE
2 cm (³/₄ in) wide, 2.5 cm (1 in) high

PROJECT COLOURWAY
Black, white and red are a classic
combination, and the high visual
contrast between the three colours
means that even from a distance small
nuances stand out – perfect for these
detailed earrings.

DESIGNER: Maria Lindemann

Owl earrings

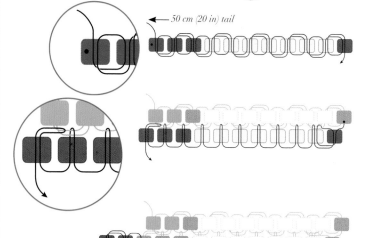

← 50 cm (20 in) tail

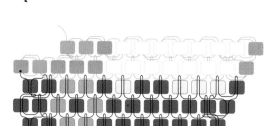

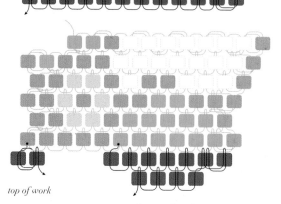

top of work

bottom of work

1 Using a 1 m (40 in) length
of thread and leaving a
50 cm (20 in) tail, ladder stitch
the following beads together:
two red, one black, seven silver
and one black.

2 Beginning with an 'in-bead'
and ending with an 'out-
bead' finish, brick stitch on one
black, seven silver and three
black beads.

3 Ladder stitch on one
red and one black bead,
looping around the last thread,
and thread through the new
black bead again so you finish
exiting the other side of it.

4 Using brick stitch and the
appropriate row starts and
ends, add the next four rows of
beads, following the diagram
on the left.

5 Finish this side of the owl,
adding the extra beads that
form the last two rows with
separate pieces at the top
and bottom of your work.

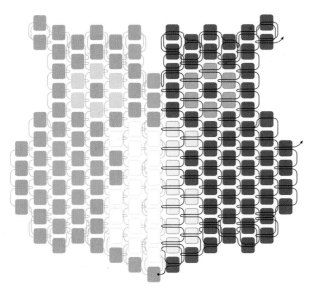

6 Return to the tail thread. Using ladder stitch, weave through all the beads in what was the first row, so that you finish by exiting the last bead added. Next, mirror all the rows from Step 2 onwards to bead the other half of the owl.

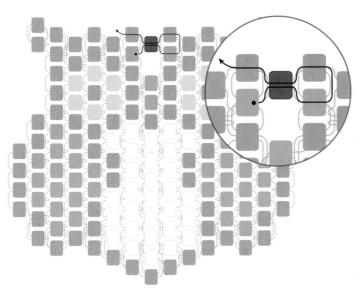

7 Weave through your work to exit the red bead ladder-stitched on in Step 3. Pick up one new black bead and cross into the black bead across the space. Weave into the red bead on this side and cross back to the black bead on the first side. Repeat all steps to bead a matching owl to complete the pair, threading the hoop earrings through the hole.

Simple brick stitch turns into a cute motif in no time at all, resulting in these irresistible earrings. Scaling up the cylinder beads to size 10s or 8s will give you a bigger owl, perfect for larger earrings or a matching pendant.

Get circling for an eye-catching pendant all around. This project works up quickly to easily make a pendant and earrings set in an afternoon.

TOOLS AND MATERIALS

★ Thread
★ Scissors
★ 22 mm (¾ in) metal ring, 1 mm (¹⁄₁₆ in) thick
★ Beading needle
★ About 20 x 3 mm cube beads (red)
★ About 20 size 8 seed beads (orange)
★ About 20 size 11 seed beads (yellow)
★ About 23 size 11 delica seed beads (green)
★ About 20 size 11 delica seed beads (blue)
★ Closed or split jump ring

TECHNIQUES

Ladder stitch (see pp.44–45)
Brick stitch (see pp.54–55)

SIZE

3 cm (1¼ in) across

PROJECT COLOURWAY

Blue, red, orange, yellow and green combine in this sunny and vibrant scheme. These primary and secondary colours always work well together to add pizzazz to any project.

DESIGNER: Amanda Preske

Circle pendant

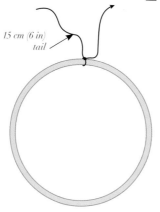

15 cm (6 in) tail

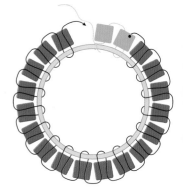

1 Tie a 91 cm (3 ft) length of thread onto the metal ring, leaving a 15 cm (6 in) tail.

2 Thread on two 3 mm cube beads and slide them towards the ring. Thread back through the second cube and pull the thread tight so that the beads sit snug against the ring.

3 Continue to brick stitch around the ring using the cube beads, passing the thread around the ring rather than around a loop of thread, as with regular brick stitch. Stop when there is space to add just one more bead.

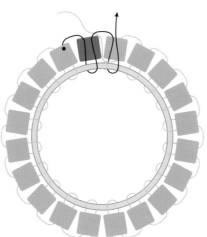

4 Add the last bead as usual, then thread through the first bead as though just adding it to secure the first and last beads together.

Hints and tips

At the end of Step 4, don't try to force an extra cube bead onto the ring to fill the gap. Instead, gently separate the beads already woven onto the ring so that they're evenly spaced out. You won't even notice once the smaller beads are added.

continued overleaf ▶

This beaded circle motif is eye-catching and appealing, and the different bead shapes and colours add interest.

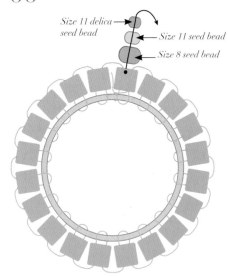

Size 11 delica seed bead

Size 11 seed bead

Size 8 seed bead

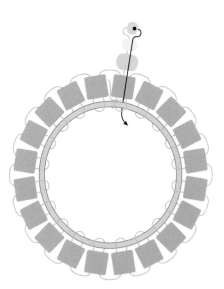

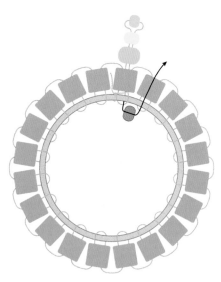

5 With the thread exiting a cube bead, pick up one size 8, one size 11 and one size 11 delica seed bead.

6 Skipping the size 11 delica bead, thread back through the stacked beads and the cube bead. Pull tight so that the new beads sit snug against the cube.

7 To add a row of beads to the inner ring, pick up one size 11 delica seed bead and thread through the next cube bead to exit the circle.

Scale back the size of this project to create a pair of coordinating earrings. Swap the cube beads for smaller 1.8–2 mm ($^1/_{12}$ in) cube beads, and use size 11 and size 15 seed beads. Using the same technique, make two miniature bead-woven circles using two 1–1.5 cm ($^3/_8$–$^5/_8$ in) metal rings and attach each to an ear hook of your liking.

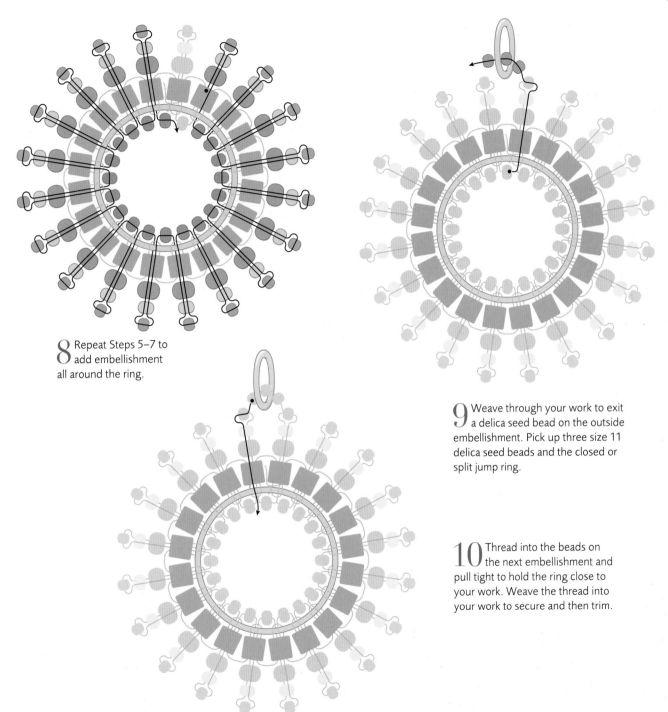

8 Repeat Steps 5–7 to add embellishment all around the ring.

9 Weave through your work to exit a delica seed bead on the outside embellishment. Pick up three size 11 delica seed beads and the closed or split jump ring.

10 Thread into the beads on the next embellishment and pull tight to hold the ring close to your work. Weave the thread into your work to secure and then trim.

Brick stitching around
a central bead leads
to an exciting ring.
The use of different
shaped and large
beads means this
works up quickly
and will adorn your
hand in no time at all!

TOOLS AND MATERIALS
★ Thread
★ Scissors
★ Beading needle
★ 12 mm round pearl
★ 1g size 11 cylinder beads
★ 8 x 4 mm firepolished beads
★ 8 x 3 mm round pearls

TECHNIQUES
Ladder stitch (see pp.44–45)
Brick stitch (see pp.54–55)

SIZE
3.5 cm (1¹/₂ in) across

PROJECT COLOURWAY
Navy blue and copper create a more
sophisticated and subtle variation of the
classic blue and orange complementary
colour scheme.

Bling ring

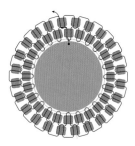

1 Using a comfortable length
of thread and leaving 15 cm
(6 in) tail, circle through the
large 12 mm pearl twice, leaving
a loop of thread on either side
of the bead.

2 Pick up two cylinder beads
and loop around one of the
loops around the large pearl and
then back through the second
bead. Using brick stitch,
continue to work around the
pearl, straddling the space
between the two thread loops
as necessary, until you have
added 24 beads. Add one more
round of brick stitch using the
cylinder beads.

3 Pick up one firepolished
bead, six cylinders and
another firepolished bead.
Skipping two thread loops, take
the needle around the next one
and go back through the last
firepolished bead. Pick up six
cylinder beads and one more
firepolished bead. Skipping two
thread loops on the base, thread
around down the next loop and
back through the firepolished
bead.

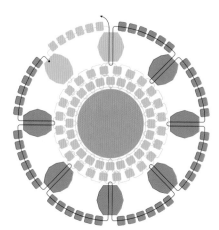

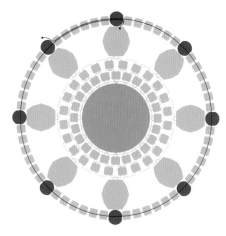

4 Repeat Step 3, adding firepolished beads
around the circle, finishing by picking up
six cylinder beads and threading down the first
firepolished bead you picked up, looping around
the thread and back down the firepolished bead.

5 Weave to the next gap between groups of
cylinder beads. Pick up one small pearl and
thread into the next cylinder bead. Repeat all
around the circle to fill in the spaces.

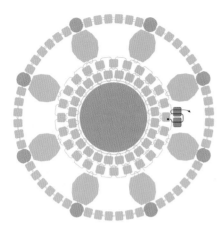

6 Weave to exit any cylinder bead on the second round. Pick up two cylinder beads and brick stitch them to the next thread.

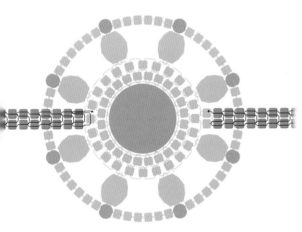

7 Repeat Step 6, adding rows of brick stitch just two beads wide until the band is long enough to fit around your finger. Finish by 'zipping' the end to the other side of the last round of brick stitch by threading into the appropriate two beads on the band, looping around the thread, and back through the second bead. Weave in all threads to finish.

Hints and tips

When adding rounds of brick stitch using cylinder beads, it may seem like too many beads at first, but be patient and they will space out as you continue to work.

The band of this ring is a simple brick-stitch strip. If you're feeling more adventurous, then you can bead it wider or use one of your own design.

The principles of this ring will work with lots of other types of beads – you will just need to adjust the bead counts.

This eye-catching ring dresses up a plain pearl with extra adornment for a bold yet sophisticated look.

Spiral rope

TECHNIQUES

Spiral rope is an endlessly variable technique which is quick to bead, making it perfect for beginners or those wanting a quick result. Due to how the stitch is constructed, it is less dependent on bead size, and so is ideal for using up beads and playing around with different sizes and shapes.

Hints and tips

Spiral rope is made up of two parts: the central core and the outer spiral.

Because you thread through the core beads at least twice, you need to ensure you choose beads with holes large enough to allow this.

For perfect results, follow the basic rules of always going in the same direction and putting the loops to the same side each time.

See pp.72–75 for this project.

Basic spiral rope

The bead sizes and quantities given in these instructions are for guidance only. Feel free to experiment with both for your own look.

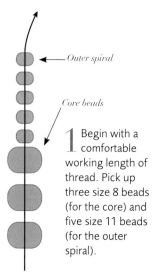

Outer spiral

Core beads

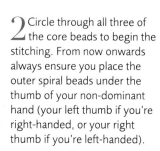

1 Begin with a comfortable working length of thread. Pick up three size 8 beads (for the core) and five size 11 beads (for the outer spiral).

2 Circle through all three of the core beads to begin the stitching. From now onwards always ensure you place the outer spiral beads under the thumb of your non-dominant hand (your left thumb if you're right-handed, or your right thumb if you're left-handed).

Double spiral

If you like spiral rope then you'll love double spiral – double the beads mean double the fun! Because you'll now go through the core beads double the number of times, you'll need to choose size 8 beads or larger. Using two different colours for the outer spiral will help you to see where you are.

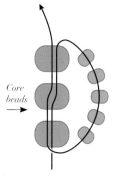

Core beads

1 Begin with a comfortable working length of thread. Pick up three size 8 beads (for the core) and five size 11 beads (for the first outer spiral). Circle through all three of the core beads and then turn your work so that the outer spiral sits away from you.

2 Pick up five size 11 beads in the second outer spiral colour. Circle through all the core beads again.

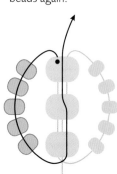

3 Pick up one size 8 bead (your core bead) and five size 11 beads (the next outer spiral) and slide these down to your work.

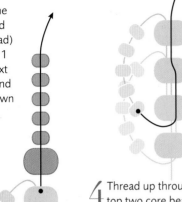

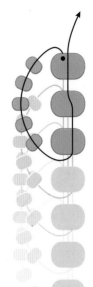

4 Thread up through the top two core beads you already had (skipping the bottom one) and then through the new core bead picked up in Step 3. This means you are again threading through three core beads, as you did in Step 2.

5 Place the new outer spiral beads (the size 11s) so that they sit under your thumb on top of the previous ones.

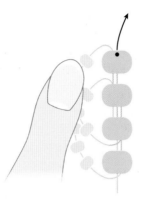

6 Repeat Steps 4 and 5 to continue the rope, adding extra length with each repeat. You always need to ensure that you thread through the top three core beads (two already there and one new one) to keep your work even.

---

3 Rotate your work so that the first outer spiral sits under the thumb of your non-dominant hand. Pick up one core bead and five of the beads you used for the first outer spiral, and slide these down to your work.

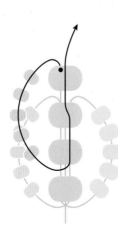

4 Circle through the top two core beads already there and the new one just added. Place this new outer spiral on top of the first one.

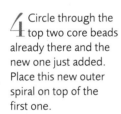

5 Turn your work so that the second outer spiral sits under your non-dominant thumb. Pick up five size 11 beads in the second outer spiral colour. Circle through the top three core beads. Place this new outer spiral on top of the second one.

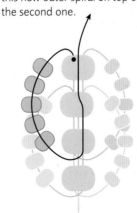

6 Repeat Steps 4 and 5 to continue the rope, adding extra length with each repeat. Note that you will only add a new core bead for every two outer spirals and only when you use the first colour.

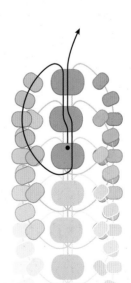

Playing with the endlessly variable simple stitch that is spiral rope gives you so many beautiful possibilities. Why not make a matching bracelet to go with this necklace?

TOOLS AND MATERIALS

★ Beading thread
★ Scissors
★ Beading needle
★ 8g size 6 seed beads in matt blue (A beads)
★ 8g size 8 seed beads in pink (B beads)
★ 15g size 8 seed beads in teal (C beads)
★ 12g size 6 seed beads in green (D beads)
★ 25g cube beads in gold (E beads)
★ S-hook clasp

TECHNIQUE

Spiral rope (see pp.70–71)

SIZE

20 cm (8 in) long

PROJECT COLOURWAY

The muted, delicate colours used here are inspired by nature and make this piece truly organic. Add a touch of originality by mixing matt and polished beads, and cube and round beads.

Spirals of colour necklace

1 Beginning with a comfortable length of thread and leaving a tail of at least 30 cm (12 in), pick up four A beads, one B, one C, one D, one E, one D, one C and one B bead.

Finishing your first step.

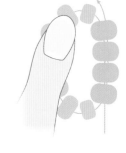

2 Circle through all the A beads to get started. This forms the first loop of spiral rope.

3 Place the other beads, which form the outer loop, under the thumb of your non-dominant hand.

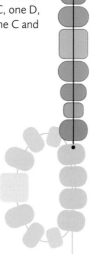

4 Pick up one A bead, one B, one C, one D, one E, one D, one C and one B bead.

5 Circle through the top two A beads added in Step 1 and the newest A bead just added.

6 Make sure these new beads sit close to the other beads and place this new loop under the thumb of your non-dominant hand.

continued overleaf ▶

Subtle complementary tones with just a hint of sparkle from the tiny gold cubes create a wonderfully textured necklace that is pleasingly weighty without being cumbersome.

7 Pick up one A, one B, one C, one D, one E, one D, one C and one B bead.

Hints and tips

If you don't like S-hook clasps, then add a clasp of your choice.

Why not double the length of the piece so that it can be worn as a long necklace or a double-stranded piece?

If after adding the loop to one end you find the necklace is too short, don't worry – you can always add extra length at the other end, since spiral rope is the same either end up.

Spiral rope is endlessly variable, as these examples show.

8 Circle through the top two A beads added in Step 1 and the newest A bead just added.

9 Make sure these new beads sit close to the other beads and place this new loop under the thumb of your non-dominant hand. Repeat Steps 6 and 7 until your work is as long as you desire.

10 Exiting an A bead at either end of your work, pick up 20 A beads and thread back into the A bead you exited. Weave around this loop and into your work as many times as possible.

11 Using the tail thread at the other end of your work and ensuring you are exiting the end A bead, pick up 20 A beads and thread back into the A bead you exited.

12 Use the two loops you have beaded along with the S-hook clasp as the fastening for your necklace.

Break all the rules
of spiral rope to make
this fabulous and
fun bracelet.

SKILL LEVEL: INTERMEDIATE

Fabulous flat bracelet

TOOLS AND MATERIALS
★ Thread
★ Scissors
★ Beading needle
★ Approximately 22 x 8 mm round pearls
★ Approximately 44 x 3 mm round pearls
★ 12g size 8 seed beads
★ Clasp of your choice

TECHNIQUE
Spiral rope (see pp.70–71)

SIZE
1.5 cm (⅝ in) wide, 20 cm (8 in) long

PROJECT COLOURWAY
Pinky copper pairs naturally with
dark blue, and both combine to create
a warm and luxurious colour scheme.

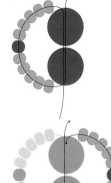

1 Beginning with a comfortable
length of thread and leaving a
tail of 20 cm (8 in), pick up two large
8 mm pearls, five seed beads, one
small 3 mm pearl and five seed
beads. Circle through the large
pearls to join into a circle, adding
this outer spiral to the left-hand side.

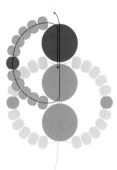

2 Pick up five seed beads, one
small pearl and five more seed
beads, and circle through the large
pearls again, this time adding this
new outer spiral to sit on the right-
hand side.

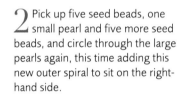

3 Pick up one large pearl, five seed
beads, one small pearl and five
seed beads. Circle through the top
two large pearls and add this outer
spiral to the left-hand side.

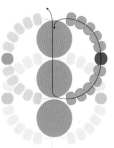

4 Pick up one large pearl, five seed
beads, one small pearl and five
seed beads. Circle through the top
two large pearls and add this outer
spiral to the right-hand side.

*Alternate outer
spirals will sit on
alternate sides.*

continued overleaf ▶

Just as with all spiral rope, this gorgeous bracelet works up quickly and provides a colourful and unusual piece of jewellery for you to enjoy. Play around with other bead and colour combinations for a whole new look.

5 Repeat Steps 3–4 until the bracelet is as long as desired, not forgetting to allow for the clasp. Pick up four seed beads, the clasp and another four seed beads. Thread back into the large pearl and weave around this thread path multiple times to secure, and then trim the thread.

6 Return to the tail thread and add the other half of the clasp, as you did the first.

← Second half of clasp

Hints and tips

It doesn't matter if you begin adding outer loops to the left- or right-hand side first. So long as you follow the same pattern as you continue, the bracelet will work.

The beads used in this project are just a suggestion. Just like regular spiral rope, these projects can be endlessly varied.

When making the bracelet continuous you need to ensure that the extra outer spirals you add carry on the pattern of lying on top of the ones below them and underneath the ones above them.

This bold variation takes a flat spiral two steps ahead by making it a continuous bangle and by adding a second row alongside the first, beaded so that it is connected to the first row. You'll need approximately 66 x 6 mm pearls and 32g size 8 seed beads.

To make the continuous double spiral

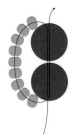

1 Beginning with a comfortable length of thread and leaving a tail of 20 cm (8 in), pick up two pearls and nine seed beads. Circle through the large pearls to join into a circle, adding this outer spiral to the left-hand side.

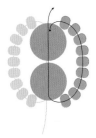

2 Pick up nine seed beads and circle through the pearls again, this time adding this new outer spiral to sit on the right-hand side.

3 Repeat Steps 1–2 until the bracelet is almost long enough to comfortably fit over your hand and around your wrist. Bring the ends together.

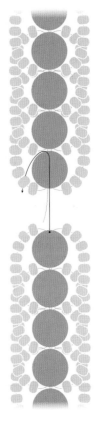

4 You now need to add two outer spirals to make the piece continuous. Weave through the first pearl added, making sure you emerge under all the outer spirals already there.

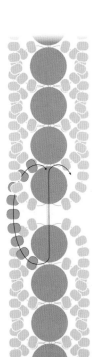

5 Pick up nine seed beads and thread into the last pearl added and the first pearl added, from the bottom up, making sure to lay the new beads on top of the last outer spirals added and to the left.

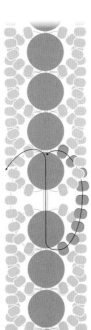

6 Pick up nine seed beads and thread into the last pearl added and the first pearl added, from the bottom up, making sure to lay the new beads on top of the last outer spirals added and to the right.

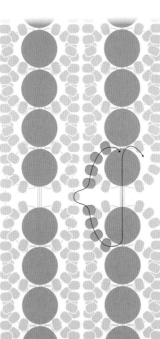

7 Repeat Steps 1–6 to bead another bracelet. However, in Step 1 when you bead the left-hand side outer loops, pick up four seed beads instead of nine, thread through the central seed bead on the right-hand loop on the first bracelet and then four more seed beads.

Adding fringes to a spiral and making it continuous brings spiral rope into a whole new world.

Spirally bracelet

TOOLS AND MATERIALS
* ★ Thread
* ★ Scissors
* ★ Beading needle
* ★ 3g size 8 seed beads in turquoise (A beads)
* ★ 8g size 11 seed beads in turquoise (B beads)
* ★ 6g size 11 seed beads in pink (C beads)

TECHNIQUE
Spiral rope (see pp.70–71)

SIZE
3 cm (1¼ in) wide

PROJECT COLOURWAY
Green and red make a complementary colour scheme, so taking it a few degrees around the colour wheel to teal and pink is always a winning combination. Both colours are warm and zing in harmony.

1 Using a comfortable length of thread and leaving a 15 cm (6 in) tail, pick up four A, five B and one C bead.

2 Skipping the C bead, thread back through two B beads.

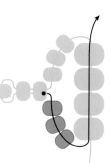

3 Pick up three B beads and circle through all four A beads.

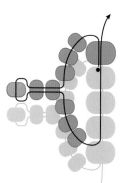

4 Pick up one A, five B and one C bead. Skip the C bead and thread through two B beads. Pick up three B beads and circle through the top four A beads to add the second outer loop.

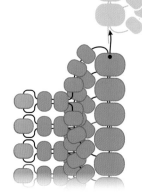

5 Repeat Step 4 until the beadwork is long enough to fit over your hand and can be worn around your wrist. Bring the ends of the rope together so that the end with the needle has the loops all pushed to the same side and the other end has them pushed to the other side.

continued overleaf ▶

Hints and tips

Just as when beading regular spiral rope, you always need to lay the outer spirals on top of each other and to the same side.

When you reach Step 11, the fringes will sit three-dimensionally on your piece and four beads should be just the right amount to sit between each one. However, pay attention as you work and if necessary, add one bead less or one bead more to keep the fringes evenly spaced.

Experiment with the length of the fringes for all sorts of results.

This fun variation on spiral rope takes the basic stitch to another level by adding fringes to the outer spirals, and then uniting those fringes to make a continuous spiral that sweeps around the bangle.

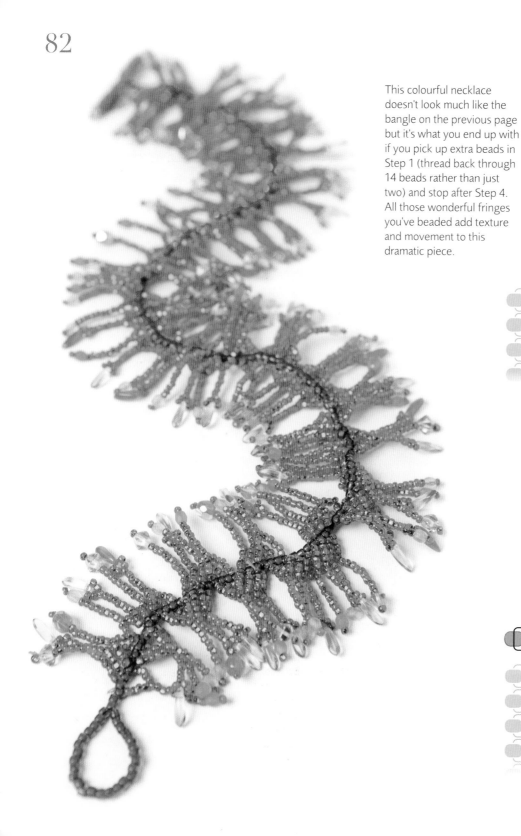

This colourful necklace doesn't look much like the bangle on the previous page but it's what you end up with if you pick up extra beads in Step 1 (thread back through 14 beads rather than just two) and stop after Step 4. All those wonderful fringes you've beaded add texture and movement to this dramatic piece.

6 You now need to fill in three outer spirals to make the bracelet continuous. The central beads are already there. To begin, thread through the first A bead added right at the start.

7 Pick up five B and one C bead. Skip the C bead and thread through two B beads. Pick up three B beads and circle through the top three A beads at the end you're exiting and the bottom two A beads at the other end.

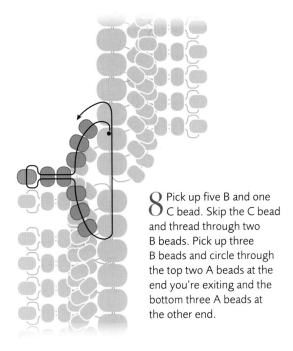

8 Pick up five B and one C bead. Skip the C bead and thread through two B beads. Pick up three B beads and circle through the top two A beads at the end you're exiting and the bottom three A beads at the other end.

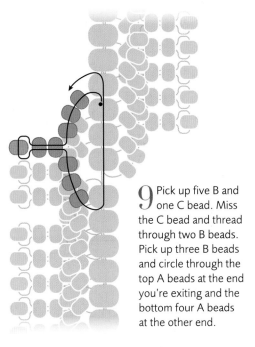

9 Pick up five B and one C bead. Miss the C bead and thread through two B beads. Pick up three B beads and circle through the top A beads at the end you're exiting and the bottom four A beads at the other end.

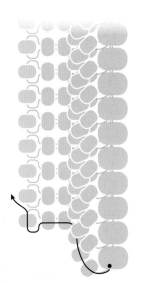

10 Your spiral is now continuous. You will find that the outer spirals you have added will move to fill in the gap and lie as needed. To begin adding the joining ridge beads, weave to exit any C bead in your work.

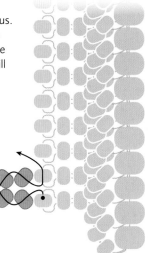

11 Pick up four C beads and thread into the next C bead at the end of a fringe.

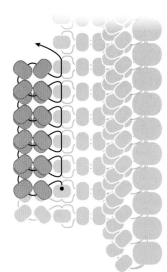

12 Continue picking up four C beads and threading into the next C bead until all the C beads at the ends of the fringes have been linked together.

Herringbone stitch

TECHNIQUES

Herringbone stitch is beaded from a ladder stitch base (see pp.44–45) using pairs of beads. Just as with other stitches in this book it can be beaded circular, tubular and spiralled, with all of these based on the basic flat version.

Hints and tips

The stitch is named for the way the beads lie in a herringbone pattern.

With herringbone stitch every time you add new beads you will need to manoeuvre to get into position to continue.

Just as with other stitches you can bead a two-drop version of herringbone stitch.

See pp.88–91 for this project.

Basic herringbone stitch

The bead sizes and quantities given in these instructions are for guidance only. Feel free to experiment with both for your own look.

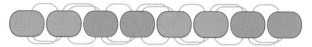

1 Begin by beading a ladder stitch base (see pp.44–45) as wide as you want your work to be – this is your first row. You may find it easier to use pairs of beads in different colours because it will help you to see which pairs you are beading on top of and where the next pair of beads begins.

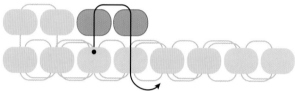

4 Pick up a pair of beads that match the third and fourth beads in the first row. Take the needle and thread through the fourth bead in the first row and pull tight.

Turning at the end of a row

The next stage in the herringbone stitch is performing the turn at the end of the row so that you can continue. There are three different methods for doing this; which one you use is up to you.

Thread outside turn

1 Simply weave around the outside edge of your work and through the last bead added in the previous row.

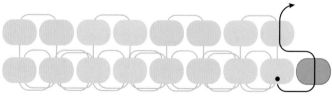

2 You can hide the thread along the edge by picking up some beads to cover it before threading through.

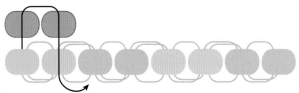

2 Using the same colour bead as the one you are exiting, pick up two beads (the first beads of the second row) and slide them towards your work. Thread into the second to last bead in the first row. This joins the new beads to the previous row.

3 Thread through the third bead in the first row and pull tight to get the beads neat. You are now in the correct position to continue.

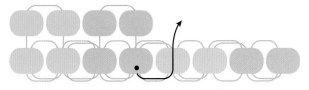

5 Thread through the fifth bead in the first row to be in the correct position to continue adding beads.

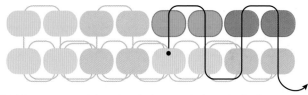

6 Making sure you pick up beads that match those in the first row, repeat Steps 4 and 5 to finish beading the row. You'll find that you finish with a repeat of Step 4.

Weaving through turn

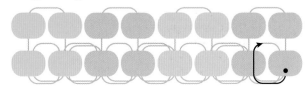

1 Weave through the next bead in the previous row.

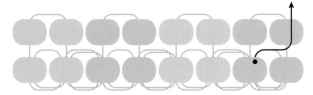

2 Weave through the last bead added in the last row.

Around a loop

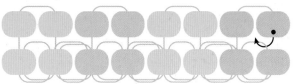

1 Take the needle and thread around the loop connecting the nearest beads in the previous row.

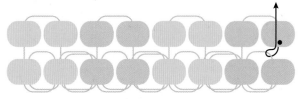

2 Weave through the last bead added in the last row to be ready to continue.

Wear your pirate allegiance on your sleeve (or blouse, or jacket…) with this skull-and-crossbones motif that has been cleverly turned into a brooch.

Pirate brooch

1 Using ladder stitch and grey beads, bead a piece of beadwork 26 beads wide.

2 Using grey beads, add four rows of beads using single-drop herringbone stitch.

TOOLS AND MATERIALS

★ Beading thread
★ Scissors
★ Beading needle
★ 2g size 11 seed beads in light grey
★ 2g size 11 seed beads in metallic blue
★ 6 cm (2¼ in) kilt pin brooch finding, with or without loops

TECHNIQUE

Herringbone stitch (see pp.84–85)

SIZE

5.5 x 5 cm (2¼ x 2 in)

PROJECT COLOURWAY

This project shuns the traditional piratey black and white for a more subtle look using matt grey seed beads combined with shiny metallic blue ones. Even though the colours are quite muted, there is still enough of a contrast between the two colours and bead finishes, which means that the motif stands out clearly.

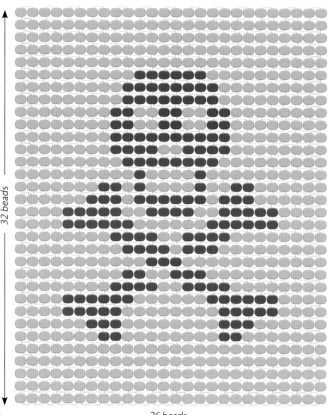

32 beads

26 beads

3 Following the chart on the left, bead the next 27 rows of herringbone stitch, making sure that you follow the chart from right to left and then left to right with every row.

4 To attach the beaded brooch to the finding, simply thread through the loops on the finding and then back into the beads. If the finding doesn't have loops, thread over the bar of the brooch. How many beads you will need to attach to the finding will depend on the size of the beads and how wide the finding is – the piece should sit nice and flat.

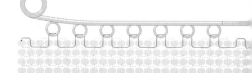

Embrace your inner pirate with this beaded motif brooch. This project is an ideal introduction to herringbone stitch and will teach you how to follow a chart while making your own unique piece of jewellery.

This necklace takes the idea of a beaded rope literally. It can be worn as a double-stranded piece or knotted for a less traditional look.

Beaded rope necklace

TOOLS AND MATERIALS
* ★ Beading thread
* ★ Scissors
* ★ Beading needle
* ★ 150g size 6 seed beads in copper (main beads)
* ★ 15g size 11 seed beads in blue (highlight beads)
* ★ Clasp of choice

TECHNIQUES
Ladder stitch (see pp.44–45)
Herringbone stitch (see pp.84–85)

SIZE
1.2 cm (½ in) wide, 104 cm (41 in) long

PROJECT COLOURWAY
The way this piece is beaded allows for some of the smaller beads to peek out and add extra interest and detail. Dark blue combines warmly with copper as they are complementary to each other.

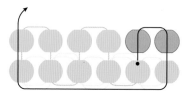

1 Leaving a tail of thread at least 30 cm (12 in), use ladder stitch to join six main beads together. Bring the ends together and stitch to join them into a circle.

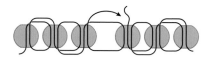

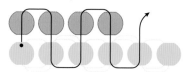

2 Pick up two main beads and thread down the next bead along, and then up the next bead along. Pick up two main beads and thread down the next bead along, and then up the next bead along.

3 Pick up two main beads and thread down the next bead along, and then up the two beads of the next stack along – the stack right at the start of your work. Note that your work will be tubular and not flat, as shown in these diagrams for clarity.

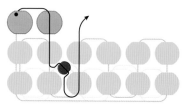

4 Pick up two main beads and thread down the next base bead. Pick up one highlight bead and thread up the two base beads of the next stack.

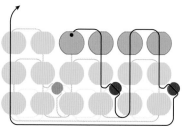

5 Repeat Step 4 twice more to finish the round, stepping up through three base beads to finish. Your work may look odd, but bear with it and in a few rounds it will start twisting.

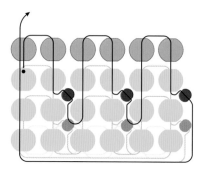

6 Pick up two main beads and thread down the next base bead. Pick up one highlight bead and thread up the three base beads of the next stack. Repeat twice more to finish the round, stepping up through four base beads to finish.

continued overleaf ▶

This bold necklace uses a lot of beads which create a wonderful height when worn. With three options on how to wear it (single strand, double strand and knotted), it is worth its weight in versatility!

Hints and tips

At first the rope won't look twisted, but bear with it and soon it will be twisting away.

Feel free to play around with any other knots of your choice for a different look.

Because of the nature of the stitch, the thread shows quite a bit, so make sure you choose one that coordinates, or even contrasts, with your beads.

7 Repeat Step 6 until your work is 104 cm (41 in), or long enough to loop easily twice around your neck. Bead one round of herringbone stitch, adding only one main bead on top of each stack.

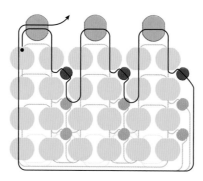

8 Weave to exit one of the three main beads added in the last round and weave through all three of them to join into a circle.

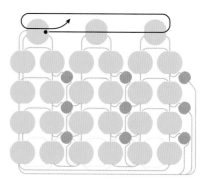

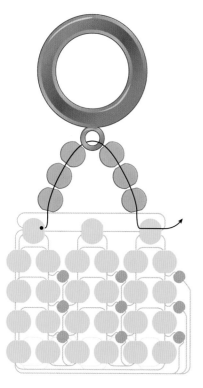

9 Exiting one of the three beads, pick up three to five main beads, thread into one end of the clasp and pick up the same number of main beads again. Thread into any of the two other main beads. Weave all through this thread path a few times to secure the clasp and then weave the thread into your work to secure, then trim.

10 Return to the tail thread and stitch one round of herringbone stitch with just one main bead at the top of each stack.

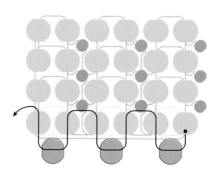

11 Repeat Step 9 on this end to attach the other side of the clasp. Weave the thread in to secure and finish.

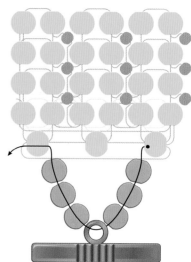

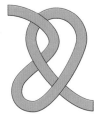

12 Your necklace can be worn as a double-stranded piece or you can tie overhand knots in the rope to mix up the look. To tie a knot, loop one end over the other at the middle of the rope...

13 ...Pull the top thread through the loop and pull tight.

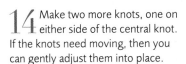

14 Make two more knots, one on either side of the central knot. If the knots need moving, then you can gently adjust them into place.

When worn knotted, this looks like a whole other necklace! You can add a single knot at the front or as many as you can fit – the choice is yours.

These beaded cones are so versatile and are great for using alongside lampwork beads or other focal beads.

DESIGNER: Eva Cadkova

Caroline beaded cones

Little beaded cones are perfect for combining with other beads.

TOOLS AND MATERIALS
★ Thread
★ Scissors
★ Beading needle
★ 0.6g size 11 seed beads in each of the 2 colours (A and B beads) per cone

TECHNIQUES
Ladder stitch (see pp.44–45)
Herringbone stitch (see pp.84–85)

SIZE
Each beaded cone is about 1.2 x 1.2 cm (½ x ½ in)

PROJECT COLOURWAY
Limes, lilacs, pinks and blues combine wonderfully in this piece as they are all of a similar tone. No colour stands out more than another, and so a harmonious scheme is created.

1 Using a 1.5 m (5 ft) length of thread, ladder stitch eight A beads together. Hold these beads close but not so tight that your work can't bend into a circle.

2 Connect the ends into a circle, then turn your work or weave so that you are facing the direction you wish to bead in.

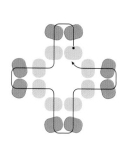
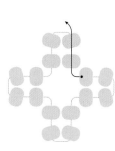
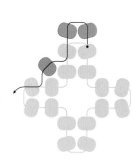
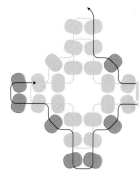

3 Using herringbone stitch and a total of eight A beads, add one round of herringbone stitch. Bead this by picking up two beads at a time and adding them to the beads added in Step 1.

4 At the end of every round you will need to step up to get into position to bead the next round. To do this, thread through two A beads: one is the next bead in the previous round and the other is the first bead added this round.

5 Pick up two A beads and thread into the top bead on the next stack as you usually would. Pick up one B bead and thread through the top bead in the next stack. This is the increase and the B bead is the extra embellishment.

6 Using A beads to bead the herringbone stitches and B beads as the increase/embellishment, repeat Step 5 three more times around your work, ensuring you step up to end the round.

continued overleaf ▶

Hints and tips

·················

To make a bracelet strung with beaded cones interspersed with lampwork beads, as shown here, you'll need to make 16 cones. For this, you'll need 9g size 11 seed beads in colour A and 9g in colour B, along with six or seven lampwork beads and a clasp. See Step 15 for more details.

·································

If you have any spare beaded cones, slip them onto simple earring wires to make a pair of matching earrings.

·································

These beaded cones are so versatile. Not only can you vary the way they are beaded, you can also use them in a wide variety of projects to create unique jewellery. Whether you use them in earrings, bracelets or necklaces, using these cones alongside lampwork beads will help tie a project together and add your very own touch.

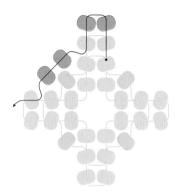

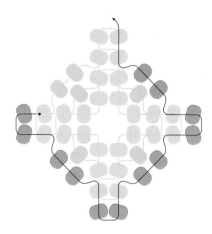

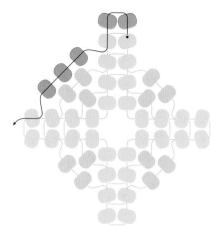

7 Pick up two A beads and thread into the top bead on the next stack as you usually would. Pick up two B beads and thread through the top bead in the next stack.

8 Repeat Step 7 using A and B beads three more times around your work, ensuring you step up to end the round and are exiting the first new bead added this round.

9 Pick up two A beads and thread into the top bead on the next stack as you usually would. Pick up three B beads and thread through the top bead in the next stack.

When deciding which colours to select to make the beaded cones, pick the three most prominent colours in your lampwork beads. Alternatively, opt for contrasting colours for bright, bold, eye-popping jewellery.

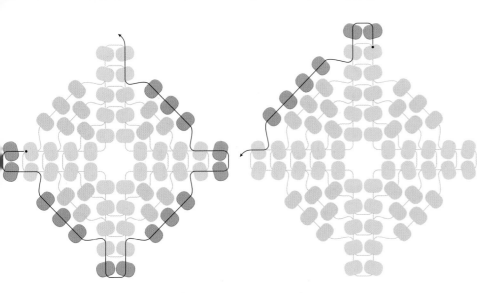

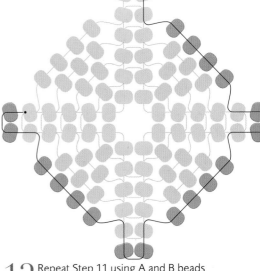

10 Repeat Step 9 using A and B beads three more times around your work, ensuring you step up to end the round and are exiting the first new bead added this round.

11 Pick up two A beads and thread into the top bead on the next stack as you usually would. Pick up four B beads and thread through the top bead in the next stack.

12 Repeat Step 11 using A and B beads three more times around your work, ensuring you step up to end the round and are exiting the first new bead added this round.

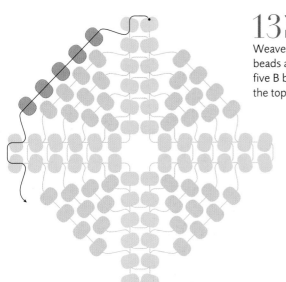

13 You will only be using B beads from now on. Weave through the first two A beads added in Step 12. Pick up five B beads and thread through the top bead in the next stack.

14 Repeat Step 13 using only B beads three more times around your work, ensuring you step up to end the round and are exiting the first new bead added this round. Weave the thread all around your work to secure and finish.

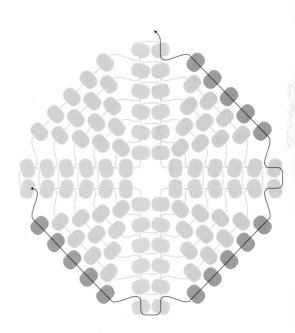

15 Stack two or three cones on top of each other to make a beaded bead, stringing a 4 mm bead in between each cone to prevent them from sliding. Fit a clasp onto one end of a length of thread, then slip on the beaded cones interspersed with lampwork beads to fit the size of your wrist, then fit the other half of the clasp.

A herringbone rope matched with dagger bead fringes results in a necklace full of colour, texture and movement.

Delicious daggers necklace

TOOLS AND MATERIALS
★ Thread
★ Scissors
★ Beading needle
★ 30g size 8 seed beads
★ Small clasp of your choice
★ Approximately 130 dagger beads

TECHNIQUES
Ladder stitch (see pp.44–45)
Herringbone stitch (see pp.84–85)

SIZE
3 cm (1¼ in) wide, 45 cm (17½ in) long

PROJECT COLOURWAY
These dagger beads have specks of blue, red, green, brown and yellow. The use of soft yellow seed beads keeps the combination warm and nature-based while tying all the colours together.

1 Using ladder stitch and leaving a thread tail of 15 cm (6 in), join four seed beads together to begin the base of your work. Join the four beads into a circle by linking the first and last beads together. Weave through your work so the needle is facing away from the tail thread.

2 Using herringbone stitch, pick up two seed beads and add them to your work. Bead another herringbone stitch using seed beads, ensuring you step up to end the round.

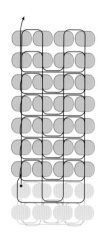

3 Continue beading herringbone stitch until the necklace is as long as you desire. Note that it will shrink as you add the embellishment, so you will need to add extra rounds later on. Also note that the following diagrams will show the necklace as much shorter than it really is.

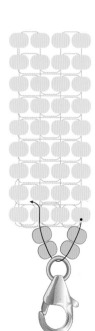

4 Return to the tail thread and pick up two seed beads, one half of the clasp and two seed beads. Thread into the seed bead on the ladder-stitched base, which is diagonally opposite where you are exiting.

5 Thread up the next seed bead to either side and pick up two seed beads, thread into the clasp and pick up two seed beads. Thread into the bead in the base diagonally opposite where you are exiting. Weave through all this again a few times to secure, then weave to exit any seed bead in the herringbone base.

continued overleaf ▶

The use of dagger beads on very short fringes creates a necklace with added drama, texture and interest. If you want a much bolder look, increasing the length of the fringes will give you the desired effect.

Hints and tips

When beading the rope, keep the tension quite loose, since this makes it easier to add the embellishment.

Not adding fringes towards the back of the necklace makes it more comfortable to wear.

You will use only seed beads for all the herringbone stitching and dagger beads purely for the fringe embellishment.

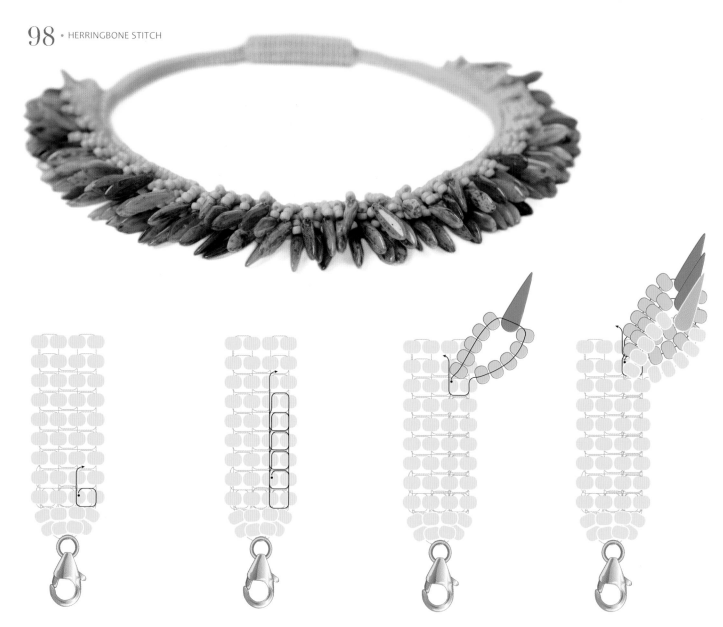

6 For Steps 6–9 you need to pull the thread tight enough so that the base is neat, but not so tight that it distorts. Thread down the bead on the same round either to the left or right of where you are (it makes no difference but use the same side each time as you go on). Thread back into the same stack you were exiting and up two beads.

7 Thread down the bead on the same round on the side you previously went down, and down one more bead. Thread back into the same stack you were exiting and up three beads. Repeat this step, which strengthens your work, until you reach where you want to begin adding dagger beads.

8 To add the dagger embellishment, exiting your work, pick up five seed beads, one dagger and five seed beads. Thread into the next stack (just as you did in Steps 6 and 7) down two beads and then up three beads in the original stack.

9 Repeat Step 8 until you have added as many daggers as desired, and then return to repeating Steps 6 and 7 along the rest of the necklace.

10 If needed, return to herringbone stitch to extend this side of the necklace, which will have shrunk as you added the embellishment, and then weave through, as in Steps 6 and 7, to tighten.

11 Add the other half of the clasp to the other end of the necklace as in Steps 4 and 5, and weave all the threads away to secure, then trim.

12 To make a clasp cover, join 10 beads together using ladder stitch, and join the ends to form into a ring. If this number of beads doesn't comfortably fit over the rope, add extra pairs of beads until it does.

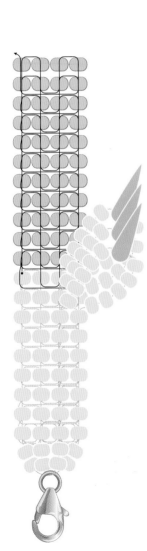

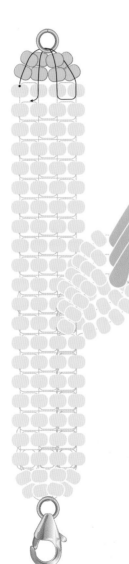

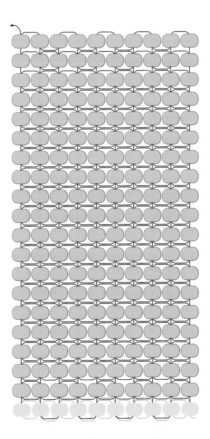

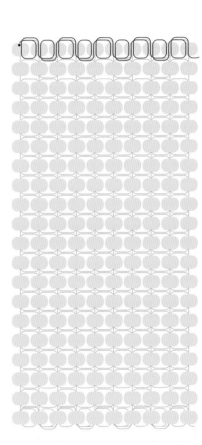

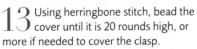

13 Using herringbone stitch, bead the cover until it is 20 rounds high, or more if needed to cover the clasp.

14 Weave through the last round as though ladder stitching all the beads together to ensure a neat finish at the end.

Adding beadwork to earring hoops means you can customise them to your own taste.

Heavenly hoops

TOOLS AND MATERIALS
★ Beading thread
★ Scissors
★ Beading needle
★ 5g size 8 seed beads in the base colour
★ 4g size 8 seed beads in the highlight colour
★ Pair of hoop earrings

TECHNIQUES
Ladder stitch (see pp.44–45)
Herringbone stitch (see pp.84–85)

SIZE
Dependent on size of hoops

PROJECT COLOURWAY
Red and cream are a classic combination, and the high contrast between the two allows the pattern to show even from a distance.

1 Thread the needle with a long piece of thread. Pick up one base bead, loop over the hoop and thread back down the base bead. Ladder stitch a new base bead to the first.

2 Loop the thread around the earring hoop and back down the new bead.

3 Continue ladder stitching on new base beads and linking them to the hoop until you have added as many pairs of beads as you desire. This is the base.

4 Using herringbone stitch, add a row of base beads, with one bead on top of every one in the base. At the end of the row, thread down two beads, around the hoop and back through two beads.

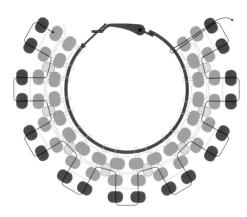

5 Add another row of base beads using herringbone stitch, but this time before you thread through the next stack, pick up a highlight bead. At the end of the row, turn as before, but this time threading up and down three beads.

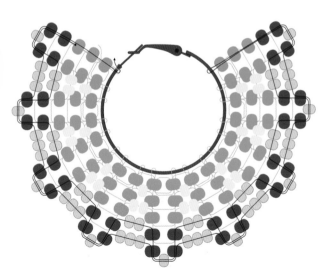

Hints and tips

Keep an eye on your work as you add the extra highlight beads – adding too many will cause your work to wave, while too few will cause it to fold in.

You can play around with beads of different sizes and shapes for your highlight beads to achieve different looks.

You can cover as much or as little of the hoop earring as you like, just so long as you add an even number of beads in Steps 1–3.

This bright variation was beaded using size 11 seed beads and no highlight beads between the stacks. For the last row, one base bead, one highlight bead and one base bead were added to each stack.

6 Continue adding rows until you have added as many as desired, increasing the number of highlight beads used each time. If you find that the highlight beads are getting too crowded, add fewer; if they are too spaced out, add more.

7 To finish the work, bead a row where you add one highlight bead onto every stack instead of two base beads. Also, add highlight beads between the stacks. Weave the threads in to finish and bead a matching earring to complete the pair.

Right-angle weave

TECHNIQUES

Named because of the way that the groups of beads sit, this stitch is the trickiest to learn, but follow the instructions and tips carefully and soon you'll be RAW-ing away!

Hints and tips

Pay attention to the circular way this stitch is beaded to keep from getting in a tangle.

Remember never to cross your work with thread – you only get into position by circling around the beads.

See pp.116–17 for this project.

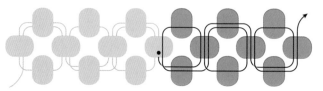

Basic right-angle weave – the first row

The first row is beaded differently than all subsequent rows because you are creating the foundation for the others to grow from.

1 Pick up four seed beads, adding a stop bead at the start if needed (see p.22). Circle through the first three beads again to join all the beads into a circle. This is the first box.

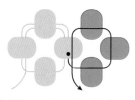

2 Pick up three beads (the second box shares a side with the first, so one less bead is needed). Circle through the bead you exited to join this second box to the first.

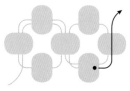

3 You now need to weave so that you are in the correct position to continue. Circle through the next two beads: the bottom/top and second side of the second box.

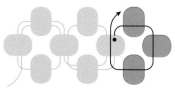

4 The third box shares a side with the previous one, so pick up three beads to create it. Circle through the side bead of the second box you exited to join the new box.

5 Once again you need to reposition to continue, so circle through two beads of the new box. Note that you are working in circular movements and you are alternately circling through the bottom and a side, and then through the top and a side.

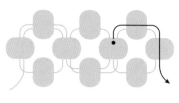

6 Repeat Steps 2–5 until your work is as wide as desired.

Subsequent rows

The next stage in right-angle weave is to add extra rows. These will share parts of their boxes with previous rows, so you'll need to pick up fewer beads for these. Note that exactly how you weave will depend on whether you added an even or odd number of boxes to the first row. The following diagrams show the different options in different colours.

If you exited facing towards the top when finishing the last box, you will need to weave through three beads to be in the correct place to continue.

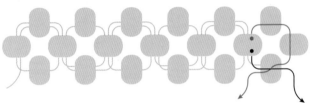

1 First you need to get into position to begin the new row. This involves circling around the last box so that you are exiting the last bottom bead added.

Whichever way you were facing at the start of this step, you need to thread through the bottom bead of the box above to attach the new box.

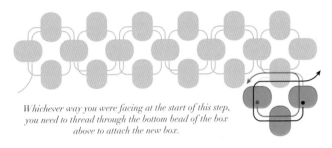

2 The first box of this row shares the top/bottom with the last box beaded. Pick up three beads and circle through the bead you exited. You have now added the first box of the second row. Note that you can now face two different ways.

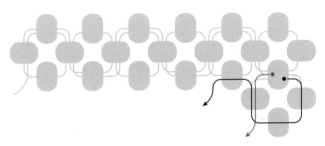

3 You now need to reposition by circling so that you end up exiting the side bead facing into your work, or the bottom bead of the next box if you are pointing towards it. The diagram shows the two options of beads to exit and directions to face.

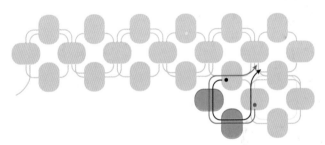

4 The next box shares a top/bottom with the box above and a side with the previous one. Pick up two beads and thread through the appropriate beads to join to the side and bottom of the previous boxes.

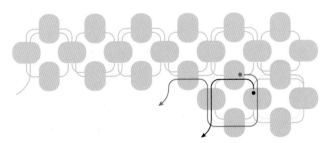

5 Reposition so that you are exiting either the side bead of the new box or the bottom bead of the next box in the previous row – whichever you didn't exit through last time.

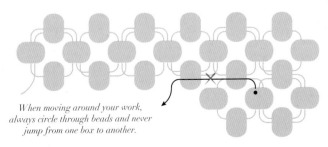

When moving around your work, always circle through beads and never jump from one box to another.

6 Repeat, adding new boxes by picking up two beads and then repositioning by circling through either one or three beads alternately when exiting the side bead of the last box added. In RAW you never cross any corners from one box to another, but always circle around them.

This four-strand braided bracelet is perfect when you want a touch of glamour!

DESIGNER: Debbie van Tonder

Fish braid bracelet

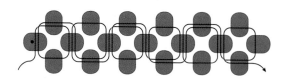

1 Using A beads and basic right-angle weave, bead a length of beadwork 35 units long, then weave so that you exit the bottom bead of the 35th unit. (Note that the diagrams show the beadwork shorter than yours will be.)

TOOLS AND MATERIALS

★ Thread
★ Scissors
★ Beading needle
★ 20g size 8 seed beads for the base (A beads)
★ 5g each size 8 seed beads in four colours (B, C, D and E beads)
★ 8-strand sliding clasp

TECHNIQUE

Right-angle weave (see pp. 102–03)

SIZE

16.5 cm (6½ in) long, including clasp

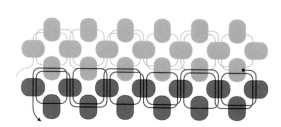

2 Continuing with RAW and A beads, add a second row to your work all the way along. This forms the base of the bracelet.

3 Weave through your work to exit the second side bead from the end of the top row. Pick up one B bead and thread through the equivalent bead in the second row of the base. The new bead should sit between the two A beads.

PROJECT COLOURWAY

Bold primary and secondary colours combine with black in this bracelet for a high-contrast look, which shows off the braiding even from a distance.

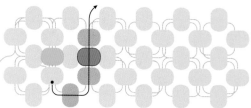

4 Weave through the base so that you are exiting the next side bead in the bottom row. Pick up one B bead and thread into the appropriate side bead on the next unit on the top row.

continued overleaf ▶

Bold multilayered beading with added braiding elevates simple right-angle weave in a clever project that has a big impact when worn.

Hints and tips

If you want to make the bracelet longer or shorter, you need to add or subtract units from the first row of RAW. Every unit added or subtracted will increase or decrease the bracelet by about 5 mm (¼ in). For instance, instead of weaving 35 units for the first row, weave 36 or 37 to make the bracelet longer, and 33 or 34 to make it shorter.

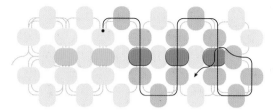

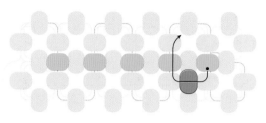

Hints and tips

Attach one unit of each strip to the clasp first and then go back to attach the second unit of each strip. This way you do not have to keep making the braid, because it is tricky to work with until attached.

5 Repeat Step 4 another 32 times until you have added a further 32 B beads. Weave through your work so that you exit the last B bead added.

6 You will now use the B beads added to form an embellishment layer of RAW. Pick up one B bead and circle through the second to last B bead added. Gently pull the B bead into place.

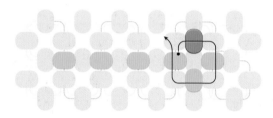

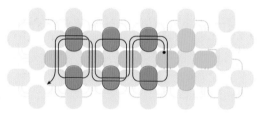

7 Pick up one B bead and circle through the end B bead. Weave through the new B bead added in Step 6 and the second from the end B bead to be in the correct position to continue.

8 Following the principles of RAW and Steps 6 and 7, continue adding B beads to create the embellishment layer. Repeat Steps 1–8 to create three more strips, this time using C, D and E beads in place of B beads.

This long slider clasp with eight loops is perfect for this bracelet – they look like they were made for each other!

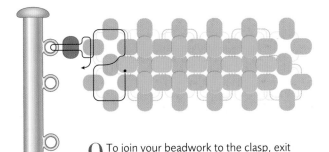

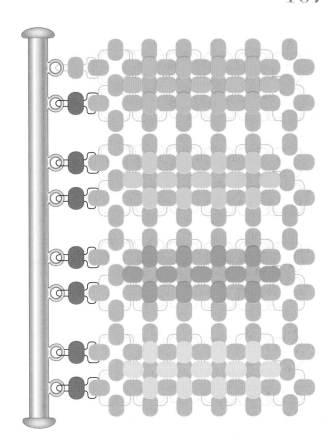

9 To join your beadwork to the clasp, exit from the end A bead of the first unit of the first strip. Pick up one A bead, pass the needle through the loop of the clasp and then back through the A bead just added and the first unit's end A bead. Repeat the thread path to reinforce the join.

10 Weave through to the second unit's top A bead of the strip and repeat. Add all the units to the loops of the clasp in this manner.

11 To form the criss-cross, bring the two outer strips to the centre and cross the strips so that the strip on the right is on top.

12 Bring what are now the two outer strips to the centre and cross the strips so that the strip on the right is on top.

13 Bring what are now the two outer strips to the centre and cross the strips so that the strip on the right is on top. Repeating the principles of Steps 9 and 10, attach the end of the strips to the other half of the clasp.

This big and bold necklace is a colourful statement piece inspired by Mexican jewellery. Beautiful acai berries that have been picked and dried from palm trees in the Brazilian rainforest are used for this project.

TOOLS AND MATERIALS
- ★ 3.2 m (3½ yards) brown or black waxed thread
- ★ Scissors
- ★ Clasp
- ★ 2 beading needles with large enough holes to take the thread
- ★ 250 acai seed beads
- ★ Thread zapper or lighter

TECHNIQUE
Right-angle weave (see pp.102–03)

SIZE
6.5 cm (2½ in) wide, 47 cm (18½ in) long

PROJECT COLOURWAY
Natural variegation on these hand-dyed acai seed beads brings variety and adds interest to the finished necklace. Acai beads are available in over a dozen different colours.

DESIGNER: Justine Standaert

Big, bold, beady necklace

1 Cut 1.8 m (2 yards) of waxed thread and attach one half of the clasp halfway down the thread. Make a double knot close to the clasp. Add a needle to each end of the thread.

2 Pick up one bead on one end of the thread and then pass the other thread end through the bead in the opposite direction.

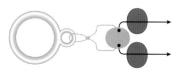

3 Add one bead to each thread end.

4 Add one bead to one of the thread ends and then pass the other thread end through the bead in the opposite direction.

5 Add one bead to each thread end. Add one bead to one of the thread ends and then pass the other thread end through the bead in the opposite direction. Repeat this step until you have added a total of 94 beads.

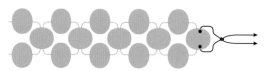

6 Make a double knot in the thread after the last bead added.

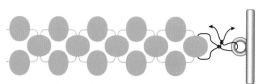

7 Tie the other half of the clasp onto the thread. Trim and burn away any excess thread. This is the necklace base.

continued overleaf ▶

Big, bold beads make for a big, bold necklace! This project takes a classic necklace design and, by using large beads, turns it on its head. If you want a more subtle look, try beading this necklace in muted pearls.

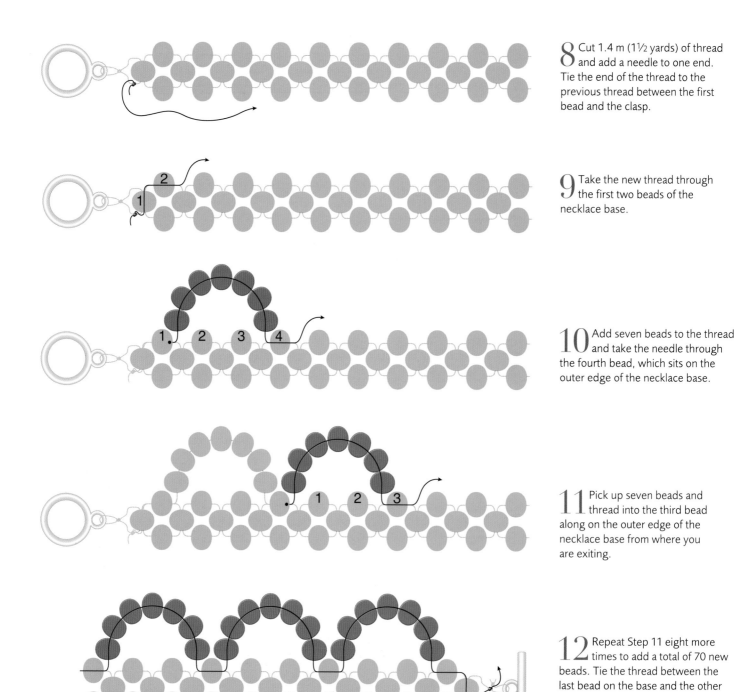

8 Cut 1.4 m (1½ yards) of thread and add a needle to one end. Tie the end of the thread to the previous thread between the first bead and the clasp.

9 Take the new thread through the first two beads of the necklace base.

10 Add seven beads to the thread and take the needle through the fourth bead, which sits on the outer edge of the necklace base.

11 Pick up seven beads and thread into the third bead along on the outer edge of the necklace base from where you are exiting.

12 Repeat Step 11 eight more times to add a total of 70 new beads. Tie the thread between the last bead on the base and the other half of the clasp.

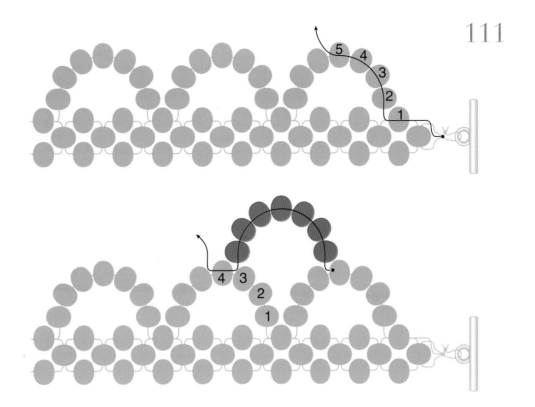

13 Don't cut the thread but instead take it through the last five beads in the opposite direction.

14 Pick up seven beads and thread through the fourth bead on the last of the loops of seven beads added in Steps 10–12. Repeat this step nine more times to add a total of 70 beads. When you arrive at the end/beginning of the necklace, make a double knot in the thread, trim it close, and burn away any excess.

Using lots of different colours – in this case yellow, orange, red, purple, green and blue – means that no single one stands out and they all combine in a riot of hues. You could also experiment with shading from one colour to another or with different shades of a single colour.

Inspired by Dorothy's shoes from the Wizard of Oz, this sparkly bow bracelet wouldn't look out of place on the red carpet!

TOOLS AND MATERIALS

★ 10 lb Fireline thread, or other strong beading thread
★ Scissors
★ Beading needle
★ 50g size 8 seed beads in the main colour (A beads)
★ 10g size 8 seed beads in the accent colour (B beads)
★ 10g size 11 seed beads to match the main colour (C beads)
★ 21 x 4 mm bicone crystals
★ Size 4 snap fastening

TECHNIQUE

Right-angle weave (see pp.102–03)

SIZE

15 cm (6 in) long. Note that the bracelet needs to fit tightly around the wrist so that the bow stays on top.

PROJECT COLOURWAY

Warm, metallic copper both combines and contrasts with the bold blue edging. The addition of sparkling turquoise crystals in the centre of the bow adds a soft touch, which visually bridges between the two contrasting colours.

DESIGNER: Shelley Nybakke

Bow-me-over bracelet

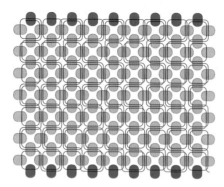

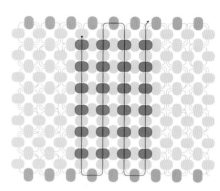

1 On a long length of thread and using right-angle weave, bead a strip of work seven units tall (for the width of the bracelet) and 52 rows wide (for the length of the bracelet). Use A beads for the body and B beads for the edges along the long sides. This strip should fit comfortably around your wrist, so add or remove rows as necessary.

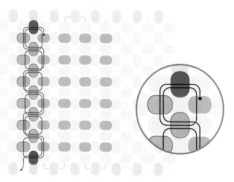

3 Weave to exit the first bead in the first column of new embellishment beads and, working off these ditch beads, add a new row of right-angle weave using A beads but with a single B bead at each end (you will do this all along the bow). This is row 1 of the bow and comprises six units.

Note: From now onwards, the diagrams don't show all of the bracelet, just the embellishment rows added in Steps 2 and 3.

2 Weave through your work to exit the fourth A bead from an edge at the top of your work (this will be a bead with its hole facing from top to bottom). Make sure you exit the bead with the needle facing towards the body of your work. Pick up an A bead and thread into the next bead along in the same column. Repeat, adding new beads across the band for a total of six beads. Weave to exit the next column and repeat beading in the ditch for the next three columns, adding 18 new embellishment beads for a total of 24.

4 For row 2 of the bow, bead right-angle weave with an increase at each end. This is done by picking up a pair of beads (instead of just one) in a spot which you will then split in the next row. When it is the first unit in a row, pick up four beads; when it is the last unit in the row, pick up three beads.

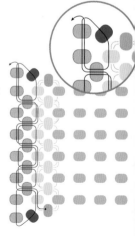

continued overleaf ▶

Wow! Advanced beading elevates right-angle weave to a higher level with this shaped and intricate bracelet. Although challenging to make, it is worth the time and effort, and is bound to draw many admiring glances.

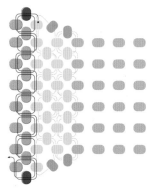

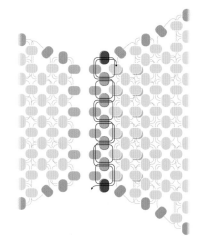

Note: The next diagram doesn't show all that you have beaded, just rows 22 and 23.

6 Repeat Steps 4 and 5 three more times so you have a final count of 14 units across. Then bead 13 rows of regular right-angle weave. You will now begin decreasing. For row 23, begin by combining the first two units in the row together when adding the first unit. Combine the next two units also when beading the second unit, and then bead the next six units as usual, combining units 11 and 12, and then 13 and 14 at the end of the row, so that you finish with a total of 10 units.

5 On this row, bead right-angle weave, splitting the increases added in Step 4 by using each extra bead to create a new RAW unit. You should now have eight units across.

7 Row 24 is another decreasing row beaded as row 23 in Step 6, to finish with six units. Row 25 is a regular row of right-angle weave. Connect the strip you have beaded to the second column of ditch-stitched beads next to the one you begun the strip from using another row of right-angle weave. Repeat Steps 3–7 on the other two columns of ditch beads for the other side of the bow.

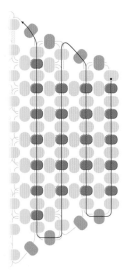

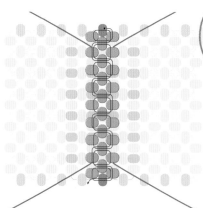

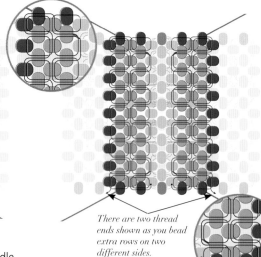

8 After completing both sides of the bow you now need to stiffen it by adding a C bead in the ditch using a new strand of doubled thread. This is beaded using the same method as in Step 2, all the way through the bow beadwork. However, on the beads that are 'joined' where you have increased and decreased, you can just go through both A beads and not split them with a C bead in the ditch if there isn't enough space.

9 Weave to exit the edge bead in the middle of where you added the four ditch rows. Using A beads, begin a new piece of right-angle weave using eight units. On the ninth unit, connect the loose strip to the middle point on the band beads at the opposite edge. This is a loose strip that is only connected to your work at each end.

There are two thread ends shown as you bead extra rows on two different sides.

10 On each side of this new strip, add two more rows of RAW using A beads for the main part and B beads for the outer edges. As you work towards the bow, it will get tighter.

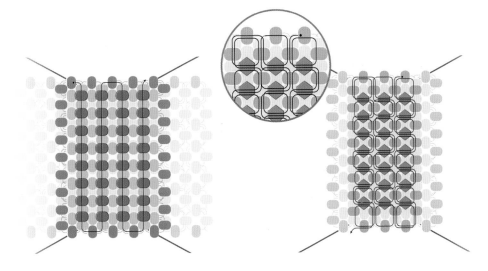

11 On this new five-unit-wide piece of beadwork, bead in the ditch as you did in Step 2. You will add four new rows of A beads.

12 Working in right-angle weave, use the beads added in Step 11 as the sides of right-angle weave units, and using the crystals, add a new layer of beadwork. Because of the bend in the strip, skip the first ditch at each end.

13 At this point add the female snap fastening to the short end of the band, which is underneath the bow, making sure you place it on the right face of the beadwork. Do not add the other half of the snap until you are almost completely finished, as you may need to add extra beadwork to adjust the length of the band.

14 Weave to exit the band one column along from where you added the ditch beads in Step 2. Using C beads, add new beads in the ditch all along the band. As you get to the end of the band, keep checking for size, as adding the beads in the ditch will contract the band; you will need to play around with this to make sure you get a proper fit. The bracelet needs to fit tightly around your wrist so that the bow stays on top, but add extra rows of right-angle weave here if needed.

15 Add B beads between each of the edge beads using a new strand of doubled thread. You need to do this prior to fitting the other half of the snap, but after beading in the ditch.

16 For added security, tack the bow onto the band near the narrow part of the bow to the side of the crystals, and also near the widest part by coming up through the band, catching some beads on the bow and back through the band. Repeat to make sure the bow is firmly attached to the band.

17 Finally, stitch the other half of the snap to the end of the band.

Get dimensional with this sparkling pendant which has a striking contrast between crystal and smooth neck cord.

Crystal tube pendant

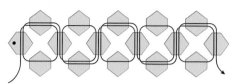

1 Using a comfortable length of thread and basic right-angle weave and the bicone crystals, bead a length of work almost wide enough that, when joined, it will comfortably fit onto the neck cord.

End of work   *Start of work*

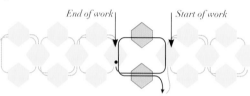

2 To join the ends, pick up one new bead and circle through the first bead added at the start. Pick up another new bead and circle through the bead you exited on the last unit and the first new bead. This is the first full round of RAW. Your work will now form a tube, but for clarity, the diagrams will show it as flat.

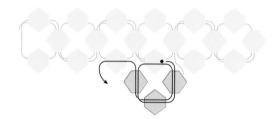

3 Begin adding a new round of RAW, beading into the edge beads already there.

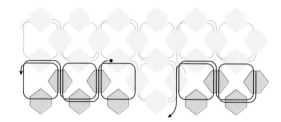

4 At the end of the round you will just need to add one bead to finish the last unit so that you are ready to continue. Repeat adding rounds until your work is as long as desired. Weave all threads into your work to secure and finish.

TOOLS AND MATERIALS

★ Thread
★ Scissors
★ Beading needle
★ 5 mm bicone crystals (you need a multiple of 10, plus an extra 5)
★ Neck cord of your choice
★ 1g size 11 seed beads (optional – see variation)

TECHNIQUE

Right-angle weave (see pp.102–03)

SIZE

1.2 cm (½ in) wide, 8.5 cm (3¼ in) long

PROJECT COLOURWAY

For this project, the neck cord you thread the pendant onto plays a big role in the colour scheme. Purple and yellow, and red and green, are both complementary colour schemes that use high contrast to bold effect.

If you want to embellish the tube with seed beads, weave to exit a bead on the outside edge. Pick up one seed bead and weave into the next crystal. Repeat all around the outside edge and then weave to the next line of crystals facing the same way and continue embellishing.

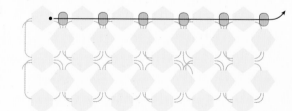

Simple right-angle weave beading appears to be made for bicone crystals, and the two combine sparklingly in this project, which lets the beads and their colours do the talking. Easily adaptable in size, scale and colour, this interchangeable pendant is bound to become a favourite.

Hints and tips

....

The large pendant is made using 165 bicone crystals; the smaller one uses 65.

....

If you'd like to add stripes or a pattern to the pendant, pay attention to which round the beads will sit on.

Combining a mix of bead sizes with some clever shaping results in this stunning heart pendant.

Crystal heart pendant

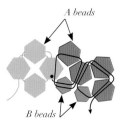

A beads

B beads

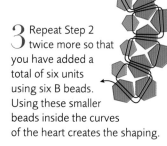

TOOLS AND MATERIALS

★ Thread
★ Scissors
★ Beading needle
★ 84 x 4 mm bicone crystals (or 5 mm for the large heart) (A beads)
★ 60 x 3 mm bicone crystals (or 4 mm for the large heart) (B beads)
★ 38 x size 11 seed beads (or size 8 for the large heart) (optional – see variation)

TECHNIQUE

Right-angle weave (see pp.102–03)

SIZE

4 cm (1½ in) wide, 5 cm (2 in) high

PROJECT COLOURWAY

You can make these hearts in a single colour, as shown here, or use two for a reversible piece. Bear in mind that the chain you use will have an effect on the finished piece. Here, a bronze chain combines just as well with the larger pink heart as it does with the smaller blue one.

1 Using a long length of thread doubled, pick up four A beads and circle through the first three to join into a circle. Weave all through the same thread path again (you will do this for every step).

2 Pick up one B and two A beads. Circle through the A bead you exited and the first two new beads. Pick up two A and one B bead. Circle through the A bead you exited and the first two new beads. In the diagrams the A beads are shown as red and the B beads as green.

3 Repeat Step 2 twice more so that you have added a total of six units using six B beads. Using these smaller beads inside the curves of the heart creates the shaping.

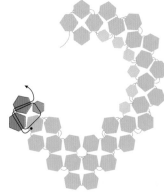

4 Using A beads, add three new units of right-angle weave. When beading the last unit, pick up the new beads, circle through the one you exited and then just the first new bead.

5 To work up the other side of the heart, add two units of right-angle weave using A beads.

6 Pick up two A and one B bead. Circle through the A bead you exited and the first two new beads.

continued overleaf ▶

Hints and tips
·················
Crystal beads can have sharp edges, so choose a thread recommended for use with crystals, or bead slowly and carefully, taking care not to pull the thread sharply around the edges of the bead holes.

Big and bold or small and subtle – the choice is yours. By simply altering the size of the beads you use, you get to determine the end result and enjoy the fruits of your labour, knowing that anyone who sees this pendant will fall in love with it instantly.

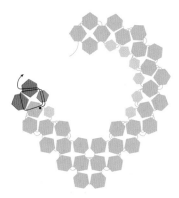

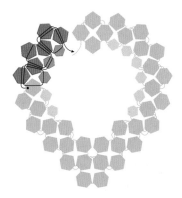

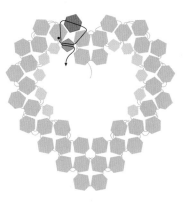

7 Pick up one B and two A beads. Circle through the A bead you exited and the first two new beads.

8 Repeat Steps 6 and 7 once more, and then Step 6 once again, so that you have added a total of five new units using five B beads.

9 You will now add the last unit that uses a B bead. This joins on to the very first unit, and it is where it is joined that gives the heart its shape. Pick up one B bead and circle through the second A bead picked up in Step 1 (it won't be the bead with the thread tail exiting it). Pick up one A bead and circle through the A bead you exited at the start of this step. Weave in all the threads to secure.

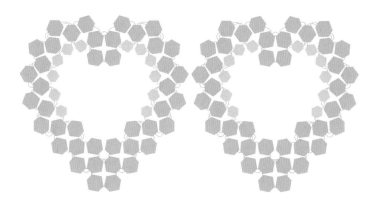

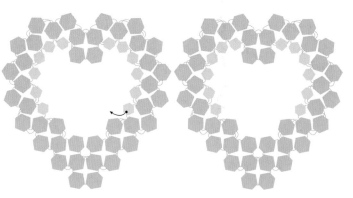

10 Repeat Steps 1–9 to bead another heart in exactly the same way. These two heart shapes form the front and back of your work and will now be joined all along the inside and outside edges using more beads. Note that for clarity, the diagrams show the hearts as being next to each other but one will be on top of the other as you bead it.

11 You will now turn the inside edge beads of each face of beadwork into right-angle weave units using new B beads. Lay the two faces you have beaded one on top of the other. Add a new thread and weave to exit any of the B beads on one of them.

If you want to add extra embellishment to your work, you can weave all along the outside edge of the heart, adding a seed bead between each crystal.

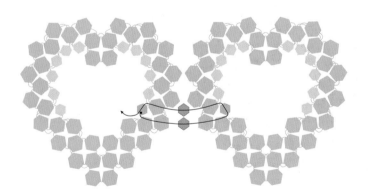

Stitch a seed bead between each crystal.

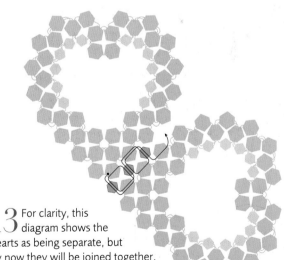

12 Pick up one B bead and circle into the corresponding B bead on the inside edge of the other face. Pick up one B bead and circle into the B bead you exited at the start of the step. Repeat the principle of adding right-angle weave units all around the inside of the hearts until fully joined.

13 For clarity, this diagram shows the hearts as being separate, but by now they will be joined together. Weave to exit any of the A beads that sit along the outside edge of one of the heart shapes and, using B beads, join the edges, forming right-angle weave units.

Combining stitches

TECHNIQUES

The stitches covered so far in this book will give you an endless range of projects, but they're not set in stone. Mixing different stitches together and combining them can give you lots more variety and scope for experimenting.

Hints and tips

Mixing stitches is ideal when you want to increase your work or make it move in another direction.

Remember that sometimes rules are made to be broken. If adapting a stitch to get the result you want is needed, then dive in.

These are just some examples of how you can combine stitches – experiment and see what others you can develop.

Peyote to brick stitch

Although they're beaded very differently, peyote stitch and brick stitch resemble each other when turned on their side. Taking advantage of this means you can easily increase along the edges of peyote stitch using brick stitch.

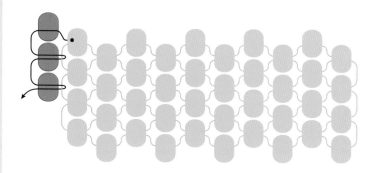

The loops of thread that join the rows in peyote stitch are perfect to add rows of brick stitch to.

Right-angle weave to peyote stitch

As you bead RAW, the gaps in between the beads are ideal for additional beading.

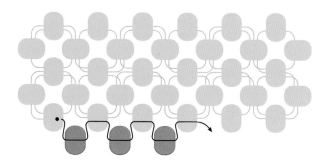

Bead a piece of RAW as large as desired and then peyote stitch new beads in between the beads that lie along any of the outside edges.

Circular peyote stitch with a herringbone increase

If you want to increase a piece of peyote stitch, using a herringbone stitch to add two beads into a space is the perfect solution. Circular peyote stitch is beaded in a very similar way to the flat, even-count version. The main difference is that you are working around in a circle and you need to step up at the end of each round.

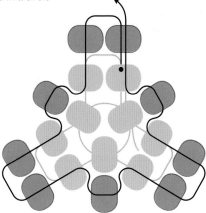

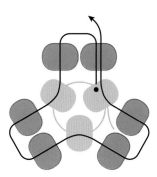

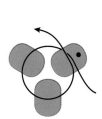

1 Pick up three beads and circle through the first to join into a circle.

2 Using peyote stitch, add two beads between each of the beads in the first round, making sure you step up at the end of the round to exit the first bead added.

3 *Using herringbone stitch, add two beads on top of the first two beads and then use peyote stitch to add one bead into the next. Repeat from * all the way around to add a total of nine beads.

4 *Using herringbone stitch, add two beads on top of the first two beads and then use peyote stitch to add one bead into each of the next two. Repeat from * all the way around to add a total of 12 beads.

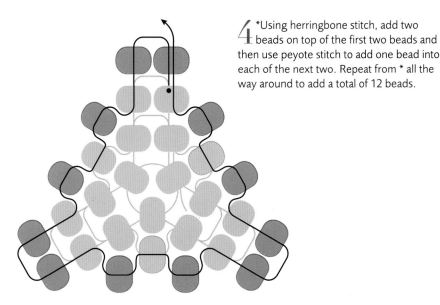

Hints and tips

Experimenting with different stitches and seeing how you can compare them will give you great results, and who knows what you will create.

Why not play around by combining stitches in other ways? For example, turn peyote stitch into right-angle weave or use peyote stitch to extend brick stitch.

A blingy ring perfect for when your outfit needs a touch of sparkle or you just want to glam up your day. Mixing peyote stitch with fringing to add embellishment to a plain ring works up in no time at all.

Riotous ring

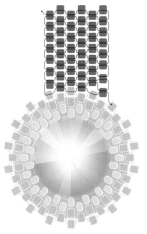

TOOLS AND MATERIALS
★ Thread
★ Scissors
★ Beading needle
★ 3g size 11 cylinder beads (A beads)
★ 1g size 15 seed beads (B beads)
★ 53 x 3 mm firepolished beads or similar (C beads)
★ 14 mm round crystal rivoli

TECHNIQUE
Peyote stitch (see pp.26–27)

SIZE
3 cm (1¼ in) across

PROJECT COLOURWAY
Shades of blue and copper combine for a warm colour scheme in this ring. Natural complements to each other, they always pair well.

1 Referring to Steps 1–9 of Rivoli medals (see pp.38–40), bezel the crystal and begin a beaded band, but peyote stitching three single beads per row when you reach Steps 8 and 9, and add the new beads to the round of A beads at the back of your work.

2 Bead the band until it is long enough to comfortably fit around your finger and has an even number of rows. Join the last row to the back of the crystal by 'zipping' it together (see p.23).

3 Weave to exit any A bead in the round nearest the back of your work. Pick up five A beads, one C and one B bead.

4 Miss the B bead and thread back through the C and four of the A beads. Pick up one A bead and thread into the next A bead along in the bezel in the same round as you're adding the embellishment to.

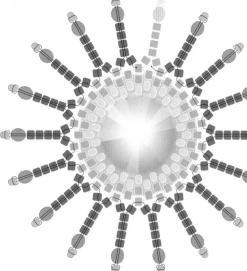

5 Repeat Steps 3 and 4 all around the band to add a total of 18 embellishing fringes.

6 Weave to exit any A bead in the centre round on the bezel. Add embellishing fringes all around this round but picking up three A, one C and one B bead to begin making each one and threading back through the C and two A beads.

7 Weave to exit any A bead in the front round on the bezel. Add embellishing fringes all around this round but picking up two A, one C and one B bead to begin making each one and threading back through the C and one A bead.

Hints and tips
....

For a more subtle look, you can just add fringes to the front round of A beads. The base ring with no embellishment is lovely to wear, too!

....

To tighten the fringes, hold the B bead and pull on the thread.

....

The diagrams from Steps 3 onwards only show the bezel and not the band you have beaded.

This dazzling ring is sure to attract attention! With its crystal centre and extra sparkle from the firepolished beads, it adds extra pizzazz to your hand.

Bold colour, geometry and a copper chain combine in this dramatic and versatile piece. It begins as a necklace and within seconds can change into a bracelet…

TOOLS AND MATERIALS
★ Thread
★ Scissors
★ Beading needle
★ 60g size 8 seed beads
★ 28 cm (11 in) chain (or more for a longer necklace)
★ 2 lobster clasps

TECHNIQUES
Peyote stitch (see pp.26–27)
Herringbone stitch (see pp.84–85)

SIZE
25 cm (10 in) long

PROJECT COLOURWAY
Use a selection of bright, rich colours for this project; the turquoise and gold palette gives a native American feel to the piece. It's hard to give exact colour quantities – it's best to use lots of colours, swapping them as the urge takes you. Clashing colours work well when combined with a neutral, such as here, where I used a grey bead for two rounds after each colour.

Thrilling triangles necklace-bracelet

1 Beginning with a comfortable length of thread, pick up three seed beads and circle through the first to join into a circle.

You must always step up at the end of every round so that you exit the first bead you added in that round.

2 Add two beads between each of the beads in the first round, making sure you step up at the end of the round to exit the first bead added. These will be the corners of your triangles.

3 *Using herringbone stitch, add two beads on top of the first two from the last round and then, using peyote stitch, add one bead into the space. Repeat from * all the way around to add a total of nine beads.

Your beadwork after three rounds: the green beads show all the beads added singularly, and the red beads are those added in pairs.

4 *Using herringbone stitch, add two beads on top of the first two from the last round, and then, using peyote stitch, add one bead into the next two spaces. Repeat from * all the way around to add a total of 12 beads.

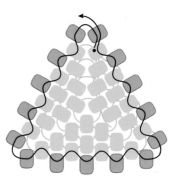

5 *Using herringbone stitch, add two beads on top of the first two from the last round and then, using peyote stitch, add one bead into the next three spaces. Repeat from * all the way around to add a total of 15 beads.

continued overleaf ➤

Hints
and tips

Watch out for the step up moving around as you decrease – it can slide to be after the corner decrease in some rounds.

I used a total of 16 different colours, changing them randomly at the end of rounds. To help unite all my colour choices, I added two rounds of grey beads between each colour.

Uniformity of shape and dimension, combined with surprising colour combinations, make this spiky necklace stand out. Hours of love and attention went into its creation... and it shows.

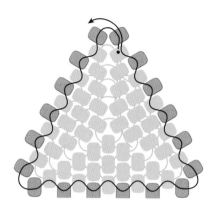

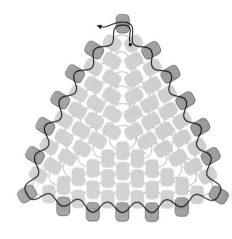

Rich, muted metallics (see above) are an inspired marriage of colours.

6 *Using herringbone stitch, add two beads on top of the first two from the last round and then, using peyote stitch, add one bead into the next four spaces. Repeat from * all the way around to add a total of 18 beads.

7 Using peyote stitch, add one bead into every space for a total of 18 beads.

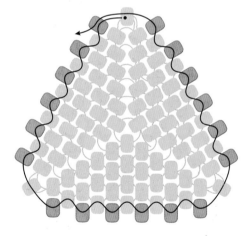

8 Using peyote stitch, again add one bead into every space for a total of 18 beads. You are now going to begin to decrease by not putting any beads in the corners. Make sure to pull your work tight as you go. Note that the diagrams now show the front side of your work greyed out.

9 Using peyote stitch, add one bead into each of the next five spaces. When you reach the next space, thread through as you normally would but with no bead on the needle. Repeat adding single beads into the side spaces and nothing in the corners all the way around to add a total of 15 beads.

10 Using peyote stitch, add one bead into each of the next four spaces. When you reach the next space, thread through as you normally would but with no bead on the needle. Repeat adding single beads into the side spaces and nothing in the corners all the way around to add a total of 12 beads.

11 Using peyote stitch, add one bead into each of the next three spaces. When you reach the next space, thread through as you normally would but with no bead on the needle. Repeat adding single beads into the side spaces and nothing in the corners all the way around to add a total of nine beads.

12 Using peyote stitch, add one bead into each of the next two spaces. When you reach the next space, thread through as you normally would but with no bead on the needle. Repeat adding single beads into the side spaces and nothing in the corners all the way around to add a total of six beads. You are now going to begin to increasing again and your beadwork will start to go out into a triangle shape again. Repeat Steps 3–12, but note that where you start each round will have moved on a space. If you want to make it easier to keep track of where you are, you can weave through to the next space so you begin in a corner, as in Step 3.

13 This is the equivalent of Step 3 but moved around one space. Add one bead into the next space and two into the next – this will be where the corners increase again. Repeat adding single beads into the side spaces and two beads in the corners all the way around to add a total of nine beads.

14 Repeat Steps 4–13 until your work is long enough to fit around your wrist, ending after Step 12 and then finishing with a round with just one bead in each of the three spaces.

15 Stitch a large lobster clasp to either end of your work and wear as a necklace by clipping each end onto a chain or clip the clasps together to wear as a bracelet.

This piece of beadwork is versatile and multifunctional. When both clasp ends are attached to a length of chain, it becomes a dramatic necklace centrepiece, but when the clasps are attached to each other, it is a bold bracelet.

This bracelet mimics the look of steel chain links with seamless rings of right-angle weave. Tightly zipped rings create links that hold their shape, but are light as a feather.

DESIGNER: Mortira Natasha van Pelt

Chain link bracelet

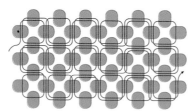

1 Cut a piece of thread 2 m (6 ft 5in) long. Using A beads, create a strip of basic right-angle weave that is three units wide and 21 units long. Weave around the final unit added to exit a bead on the edge of a short side. Weave in and trim the tail (note that the diagrams show the beadwork shorter than it actually is).

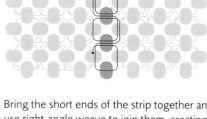

2 Bring the short ends of the strip together and use right-angle weave to join them, creating three new units. Use strong, consistent tension to ensure even beadwork throughout the ring.

TOOLS AND MATERIALS
★ Strong beading thread
★ Scissors
★ Beading needle
★ 30–40g size 11 seed beads in two colours (A and B beads)

TECHNIQUES
Peyote stitch (see pp.26–27)
Right-angle weave (see pp.102–03)

SIZE
A nine- or ten-link chain will create a bracelet about 18 cm (7 in) long

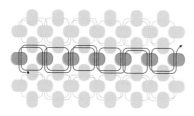

3 Use the same zipping method to connect the long sides of the right-angle weave strip. As the edges are drawn together, a sturdy ring shape will form. Exit from a bead at the edge of the circular strip, pick up one bead and stitch through the opposite edge bead on the other side. Pull snug and gently fold the edges together.

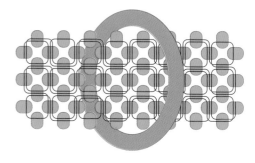

4 Using B beads, bead a new strip of right-angle weave the same size as the first. Pass this strip through the first ring and join the short edges together. If you ever forget to link the new strip before zipping it together you can always zip up a new panel with two rings attached, although this becomes more complicated if you are using more than two colours in a pattern.

Tip
When you reach the final few stitches, gently elongate the bead ring, so that the final gap is centred on a long side. This will help bring the final few beads together more neatly.

5 Continue adding new rings to the chain until it has almost reached the desired length.

continued overleaf ▶

Altering
the ring sizes

....

*You can add a few more rows to the basic
RAW panels to make slightly larger rings for a
softer necklace, for instance. But remember that
the longer the beadwork, the more flexible and
bendy the rings will become. If the rings are too
large, they won't hold the distinctive oblong shape
of traditional chain links. Reducing the size of
the RAW rings is not recommended; any
smaller, and there isn't enough 'stretch'
room to zip up the seams.*

Shown here worn as a
bracelet, you can just
add as many or as few
links as needed for
the desired length.
Because the toggle fits
any of the links, you
can adjust the length
of the chain as desired,
and even make an
extra-long chain for
a slinky belt!

6 Now make the toggle. Using a long length of thread with a stop bead on it, pick up an even number of seed beads (approximately 20) in the next colour of your pattern. The beaded length should roughly match the length of a beaded ring when elongated. Slide the beads down to the stop bead.

7 Using even-count peyote stitch, create a piece of beadwork eight rows long. You will know it is long enough when there are four beads along each edge. Weave in the tail and trim.

8 Bring the first and last rows of your beadwork together and zip up to form a tube. Note that for clarity, the diagrams now show your work flat but in reality it is a tube.

9 Weave through the tube so that you are exiting an edge bead. Pick up three beads to begin forming a picot decoration. Thread into the next bead along on the edge. Weave up to exit the next edge bead in the tube. Note that the picot beads are a different colour in the diagram, but you can bead them to match the tube.

10 Pick up three beads and stitch down into the next edge bead. Weave up through to exit the next edge bead again and the first picot bead above it.

11 Pick up one bead and thread down into the next picot bead of the other group of three and the following edge bead. Weave to exit the next edge bead along, then add another bead between two picots, as before, to complete the pattern. Stitch through all four of the top picot beads to cinch them closed, then pass down into the tube.

12 Weave to the other end of the tube and repeat Steps 9–11 to embellish this end as well.

Because each link in the chain is stitched separately, there are many possibilities for colour patterns. You can make every link a different colour for a rainbow or ombré (multicoloured) effect. For a minimalist design, make every link the same, but with a single link in a contrasting colour.

Hints and tips

This project can be worked using the thread of your choice; however, a fused or braided beading thread will provide a 'hardness' to the links, allowing them to mimic real chain and make a sturdy, chunky bracelet.

Always test the size of the bracelet on your wrist or a bracelet sizing cone before finishing. The shape of the rings and the way they connect can make length deceiving.

Test the length of the bracelet on your wrist before securing the toggle. You can add extra beads to the loop to increase the length by a few millimeters, but when possible, add more links rather than an extra-long clasp.

13 Weave through the tube to exit from the centre. Pick up enough beads (approximately 20) to wrap around one of the chain links. Pass back through the first three beads added and into the peyote tube. Weave all around the loop twice more to strengthen, then secure the thread and trim. The toggle is now finished.

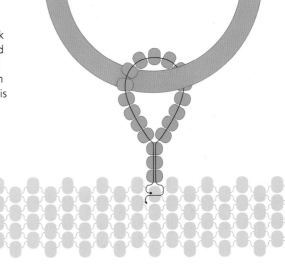

These earrings are perfect for when you want a touch of sparkle! Quick to bead, they'll add a touch of elegance to your wardrobe.

TOOLS AND MATERIALS

★ Thread
★ Scissors
★ Beading needle
★ 1g size 11 seed beads (A beads)
★ 5g size 15 seed beads (B beads)
★ 48 x 4 mm bicone crystals (C beads)
★ Pair of ear wires

TECHNIQUES

Peyote stitch (see pp.26–27) and Right-angle weave (see pp.102–03)

SIZE

About 2.5 cm (1 in), without ear wires

PROJECT COLOURWAY

Red and coppery gold create a warm scheme that has a touch of sophistication without too much contrast.

DESIGNER: Juanita Carlos

Crystal earrings

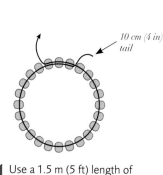

10 cm (4 in) tail

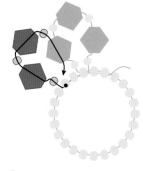

1 Use a 1.5 m (5 ft) length of thread, leaving a 10 cm (4 in) tail to weave in later. Pick up 24 A beads and circle through the first three beads. This is the base circle.

2 Pick up one B, one C, one B, one C, one B, one C and one B bead. Circle through the A bead you are exiting then the next two A beads in the base circle.

3 Pick up one B, one C, one B, one C and one B bead. Thread through the first C bead added in Step 2 to join this new loop of beads to the first one added in Step 2.

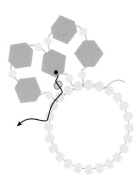

4 Pick up one B bead and circle through the A bead you were exiting and the next two A beads in the base circle.

5 Repeat Step 3 and 4 nine more times to add a total of 24 crystals to your beadwork.

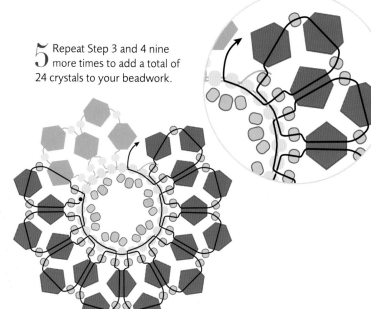

continued overleaf ▶

These earrings are large enough to notice, but small enough not to overpower your face or outfit.

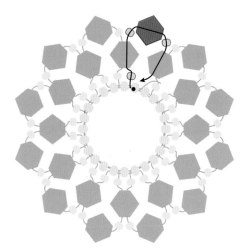

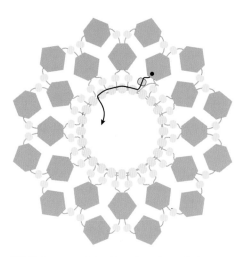

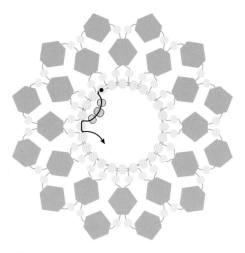

6 Pick up one B bead. Thread through the next C bead (the third picked up in Step 2). Pick up one B, one C and one B bead. Thread through the last crystal added in Step 5.

7 Pick up one B bead and go through the A bead you exited at the start of this step and then the next three A beads in the base circle.

8 You will now bead inside the base circle. Pick up one B, one A and one B bead. Miss the next three A beads in the base circle and go through the next.

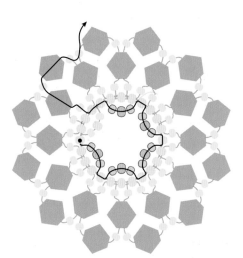

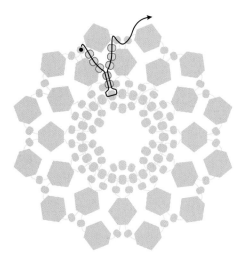

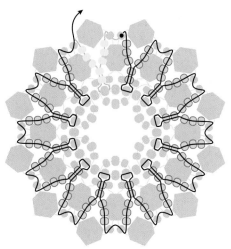

9 Repeat Step 8 five more times to add a total of six loops of beads. To finish, thread through the A bead you exited at the start of Step 7, the next A, B, C, B, C and the next two B beads.

10 From now on, the beadwork you have created so far will be shown in grey, for clarity. Pick up five B beads. Thread into the A bead beneath the next step of three crystals. Thread through the last two B beads just added and pick up three B beads. Thread through the next two B beads between the next two outer C beads.

11 Repeat Step 10 eleven more times to add loops all around, and finish by exiting the two B beads you exited at the start of Step 10.

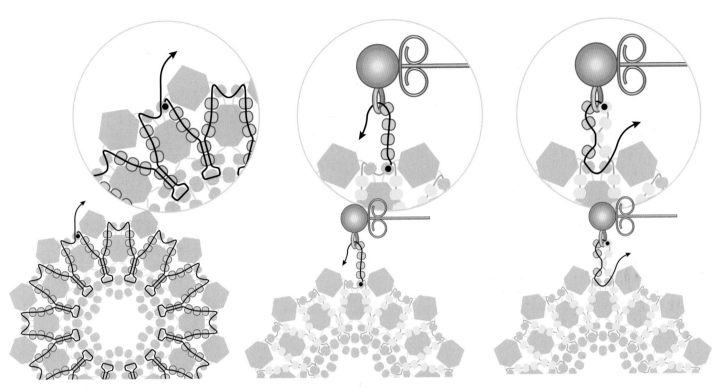

12 You will now embellish the other side of the earring, so turn it over. Repeat Steps 10 and 11, adding loops of beads and finishing by exiting two B beads.

13 Lastly, form the loop to hang the earring from. Making sure you hold the earring so the right side faces outward, pick up four B beads and thread through the loop of the ear wire.

14 Pick up two B beads and thread through the second B bead added in Step 13. Pick up one B bead and circle through the two B beads you exited at the start of Step 13. Repeat the thread path to reinforce it. Repeat Steps 1–14 to make a matching earring.

Red and gold is a classic combination, creating a sumptuous, ornate look with hints of the Orient.

Get creative and three-dimensional with this cute beaded creature! Ralph can be used as a pendant, charm or ornament.

TOOLS AND MATERIALS
★ Thread
★ Scissors
★ Beading needle
★ 8g size 11 cylinder beads in grey (A beads)
★ 12 x size 11 cylinder beads in pink (B beads)
★ 2 x 2 mm round beads in black (C beads)
★ 1 small drop bead in black (D bead)
★ 3 cm (1¼ in) wooden bead
★ Closed jump ring (if making into a pendant)

TECHNIQUES
Peyote stitch (see pp.26–27)
Brick stitch (see pp.54–55)

SIZE
7 cm (2¼ in) wide, 3 cm (1¼ in) high

DESIGNER: Shirley Lim

Ralph the rat

1 You will need about 4.5 m (5 yards) of thread. Begin by unwinding half this amount from the bobbin and use that. When you return to the start (in Step 7), unwind the rest of the thread needed. Pick up 76 A beads, which will be rows 1 and 2 for the top and bottom of the beaded bead (common rows). Pass the needle through the 76 beads one more time and through the first bead again. At the end of every round you must step up to thread through the first new bead added in that round.

2 **Rows 3–4:** Bead two rows of peyote stitch using A beads. **Row 5:** Peyote stitch using five A beads, one C bead, two A beads, one C bead and 29 A beads. **Row 6:** Peyote stitch using A beads.

3 **Row 7:** Peyote stitch with one A bead in 15 spaces, then decrease in the next space by weaving through your work so that you don't add a bead in the next space. Peyote stitch with one A bead in 18 spaces, then decrease in the next space by weaving through your work so that you don't add a bead in the next space. Peyote stitch with one A bead in the last three spaces.

4 **Row 8:** Peyote stitch using one A bead in the next 14 spaces. Add two A beads in the next space. Peyote stitch using one A bead in the next 17 spaces. Add two A beads in the next space. Peyote stitch with one A bead in the last three spaces.

5 **Row 9:** Peyote stitch using one A bead in the next 14 spaces. Pass through two beads. Peyote stitch using one A bead in the next 18 spaces. Pass through two beads. Peyote stitch with one A in the last four spaces.

continued overleaf ▶

These cute beaded heads take their inspiration from the Chinese zodiac, a 12-year mathematical cycle in which each year is represented by an animal.

6 Bead the following, always with peyote stitch, and increase and decrease as indicated:

Row 10: Peyote stitch with 36 x 1A.
Row 11: Peyote stitch with 36 x 1A.
Row 12: *Perform a decrease, peyote stitch with 5 x 1A. Repeat from * six times to finish the round.
Row 13: *Peyote stitch with 4 x 1A. Pick up 2 A beads and pass through the next bead. Repeat from * six times to finish the round.
Row 14: Peyote stitch with 4 x 1A. *Pass through 2 A beads. Peyote stitch with 5 x 1A. Repeat from * five times. Pass through 2 As and 1A.
Row 15: Peyote stitch with 30 x 1A.
Row 16: Peyote stitch with 30 x 1A.
Row 17: Peyote stitch with 2 x 1A. *Perform a decrease. Peyote stitch with 4 x 1A. Repeat from * five times. Perform a decrease and peyote stitch with 2 x 1A.
Row 18: Peyote stitch with 24 x 1A.
Row 19: Peyote stitch with 24 x 1A.
Row 20: *Perform a decrease. Peyote stitch with 3 x 1 A. Repeat from * six times.
Row 21: Peyote stitch with 18 x 1A.
Row 22: Peyote stitch with 18 x 1A.
Row 23: Peyote stitch with 1 x 1A. *Perform a decrease. Peyote stitch with 2 x 1A. Repeat from * five times. Perform a decrease. Peyote stitch with 1 x 1A.
Row 24: Peyote stitch with 12 x 1A.
Row 25: Peyote stitch with 12 x 1A.
Row 26: *Peyote stitch with 1 x 1A. Perform a decrease. Repeat from * six times.
Row 27: Peyote stitch with 6 x 1A.
Row 28: Peyote stitch with 6 x 1A.
Pass the needle through the last rows twice more to strengthen them. Weave the thread into your work to secure and trim.

7 Return to the start and unwind the rest of the thread to bead the bottom half of the head. Beading into the first rows you added, bead the following:

Row 3: Peyote stitch with 38 x 1A.
Row 4: Peyote stitch with 38 x 1A.
Row 5: Peyote stitch with 28 x 1A, 1 x D and 1 x 9A. Insert the wooden bead into your work.
Row 6: Peyote stitch with 18 x 1A. Perform a decrease. Peyote stitch with 18 x 1A. Perform a decrease. Peyote stitch with 38 x 1A. Perform a decrease.
Row 7: *Peyote stitch with 17 x 1A. Pick up 2 A beads and pass through the next bead. Repeat from * twice.
Row 8: Peyote stitch with 17 x 1A. *Pass through 2 A beads. Peyote stitch with 18 x 1A. Pass through 2 A beads. Peyote stitch with 1 A bead.
Row 9: Peyote stitch with 36 x 1A.
Row 10: Peyote stitch with 36 x 1A.
Row 11: Peyote stitch with 3 x 1A. *Perform a decrease. Peyote stitch with 5 x 1A. Repeat from * five times. Perform a decrease and peyote stitch with 2 x 1A.
Row 12: Peyote stitch with 2 x 1A. *Pick up 2 A beads and pass through the next bead. Peyote stitch with 4 x 1A. Repeat from * five times. Pick up 2 A beads and pass through the next bead. Peyote stitch with 2 x 1A.
Row 13: Peyote stitch with 2 x 1A. *Pass through 2 A beads. Peyote stitch with 5 x 1A. Repeat from * five times. Pass through 2 A beads. Peyote stitch with 3 x 1A.
Row 14: Peyote stitch with 30 x 1A.
Row 15: Peyote stitch with 30 x 1A.
Row 16: *Perform a decrease. Peyote stitch with 4 x 1A. Repeat from * six times.
Row 17: *Peyote stitch with 3 x 1A. Pick up 2 A beads and pass through the next bead. Repeat from * six times.

Hints and tips

To help prevent the thread from tangling, you may want to wax it or use thread conditioner before you start beading.

Ralph is beaded mainly using peyote stitch, with brick stitch used for the ears.

You will start stitching from the centre of the wooden bead towards the top of the head and then return to the starting rows and bead the bottom of the head.

Row 18: Peyote stitch with 3 x 1A. *Pass through 2 A beads. Peyote stitch with 4 x 1A. Repeat from * five times. Pass through 2 A beads. Peyote stitch with 1A.
Row 19: Peyote stitch with 24 x 1A.
Row 20: Peyote stitch with 24 x 1A.
Row 21: Peyote stitch with 1A. *Perform a decrease. Peyote stitch with 3 x 1A. Repeat from * five times. Perform a decrease and peyote stitch with 2 x 1A.
Row 22: Peyote stitch with 18 x 1A.
Row 23: Peyote stitch with 18 x 1A.
Row 24: *Peyote stitch with 2 x 1A. Perform a decrease. Repeat from * six times.
Row 25: Peyote stitch with 12 x 1A.
Row 26: Peyote stitch with 12 x 1A.
Row 27: *Perform a decrease. Peyote stitch with 1A. Repeat from * six times.
Row 28: Peyote stitch with 6 x 1A.
Row 29: Peyote stitch with 6 x 1A.
Pass the needle through the last rows two more times to strengthen. Weave through your work to secure the thread and then trim.

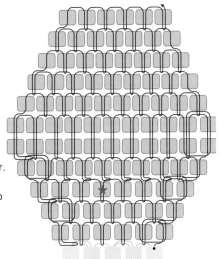

8 To begin the ears: ladder stitch 1 x A, 3 x B and 1 x A beads together.

9 Using single and two-drop brick stitch and the appropriate starts and ends, bead the next 12 rows of the ear. Note that row 4 has increases where you will add two beads to the same space. The extra bead is indicated with a red star. Row 6 is beaded using two-drop brick stitch.

10 Using six A beads to cover the thread at the top of the ear, weave through your work, adding the new beads to the last row. Repeat Steps 8–10 to bead the second ear.

11 To attach the ears, weave from the head into a bead on the ear, back into the head and back into the next bead in the ear, etc. Using the tail thread, pass the needle into row 5 of the head (this is the same row as the eyes) into the eighth bead away from one of the eyes pointing towards the front of the head.

12 Pass the needle into one of the end A beads on the ladder stitch row of one of the ears. Weave to the second bead on the same row and stitch into the head again. Continue weaving back and forth until fully attached, stitching the ear upwards. Weave in the thread to secure, trim and repeat for the other ear.

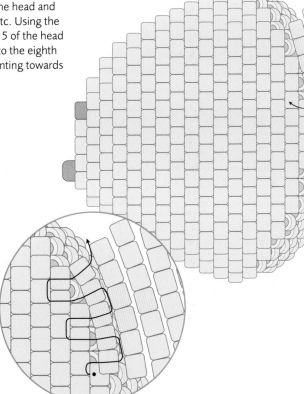

Hints and tips

To turn Ralph into a pendant, weave to exit a bead in the last row at the top of the head, then pick up a small number of A beads or small seed beads, plus a closed jump ring and thread into a bead on the opposite side of the last row. Weave back through again to secure.

Resources

UNITED KINGDOM

Beadworks UK Ltd
Gemstones, pearls, vermeil, threading
materials, tools
www.beadworks.co.uk

Bead Cornucopia
Beads, pearls, charms and pendants,
findings, stringing materials
www.beadsandjewellerysupplies.co.uk

Beads Direct
Semiprecious beads, Shamballa beads,
findings, chains, wire
www.beadsdirect.co.uk

Bijoux Beads
Beads, findings and components,
cords, threads and wire, kits
www.bijouxbeads.co.uk

Cookson Gold
Beads, kits, storage, tools, stringing
materials
www.cooksongold.com

Hobbycraft
Beads, findings, threading materials,
jewelry-making equipment
www.hobbycraft.co.uk

International Craft
Wholesale beads and jewelry-making
supplies
www.internationalcraft.com

London Jewellery Supplies
Beads, tools, findings, threading
materials
www.londonjewellerysupplies.co.uk

Spoilt Rotten
Beads and charms, components,
jewelry kits, tools
www.spoiltrottenbeads.co.uk

The Bead Shop
Beads, stringing materials, findings
www.the-beadshop.co.uk

The Spellbound Bead Company
Beads, wire, findings, tools
www.spellboundbead.co.uk

Index

Acknowledgments

Author acknowledgments: I would like to
express my gratitude to the many people who
helped this book come into existence, especially the
guest designers who kindly shared their work.
In addition, a great big thank you to my family,
including my beading family spread across the world,
and he who knows who he is for not grumbling too
much as he vacuums up all the beads I've dropped.

Publisher acknowledgments: Quarto would
like to thank MOT Models and Zone Models.